BestMasters

Springer awards „BestMasters" to the best master's theses which have been completed at renowned universities in Germany, Austria, and Switzerland.

The studies received highest marks and were recommended for publication by supervisors. They address current issues from various fields of research in natural sciences, psychology, technology, and economics.

The series addresses practitioners as well as scientists and, in particular, offers guidance for early stage researchers.

Christoph Samitsch

Data Quality and its Impacts on Decision-Making

How Managers can benefit from Good Data

Christoph Samitsch
Innsbruck, Austria

Master's thesis, Management Center Innsbruck 2014, Innsbruck, Austria

BestMasters
ISBN 978-3-658-08199-7   ISBN 978-3-658-08200-0 (eBook)
DOI 10.1007/978-3-658-08200-0

Library of Congress Control Number: 2014956117

Springer Gabler
© Springer Fachmedien Wiesbaden 2015
This work is subject to copyright. All rights are reserved by the Publisher, whether the whole or part of the material is concerned, specifically the rights of translation, reprinting, reuse of illustrations, recitation, broadcasting, reproduction on microfilms or in any other physical way, and transmission or information storage and retrieval, electronic adaptation, computer software, or by similar or dissimilar methodology now known or hereafter developed.
The use of general descriptive names, registered names, trademarks, service marks, etc. in this publication does not imply, even in the absence of a specific statement, that such names are exempt from the relevant protective laws and regulations and therefore free for general use.
The publisher, the authors and the editors are safe to assume that the advice and information in this book are believed to be true and accurate at the date of publication. Neither the publisher nor the authors or the editors give a warranty, express or implied, with respect to the material contained herein or for any errors or omissions that may have been made.

Printed on acid-free paper

Springer Gabler is a brand of Springer Fachmedien Wiesbaden
Springer Fachmedien Wiesbaden is part of Springer Science+Business Media
(www.springer.com)

Foreword

For all types of businesses, there is an increasing trend towards the utilization of data, as well as information that can be gathered from data. Big Data or Data Scientist are the new terms that emerged from recent developments in the field of data and information science, just to mention a couple examples.

The assurance of data quality has become an integral part of information management practices in organizations. Data of high quality may be the basis for making good decisions, whereas poor data quality may have negative effects on decision-making tasks. This will eventually lead to the need for changing requirements for decision support systems (DSS). In particular, it will change the way data is being gathered and presented in order to aid decision-makers.

After a thorough literature review on the topic of data and information quality, fields of research that are deemed relevant for this research project could be classified. What really stands out from this literature review is the concept of data quality dimensions, whereby the goal of this research project was to measure the degree to which each of these dimensions has an effect on decision-making quality.

An experiment was conducted as the methodology to collect data for this research project. From the data collected, the research questions could be answered, and a conclusion could be drawn. The experiment was broken down into five treatment groups, each of which had to go through a specific scenario and complete tasks. The purpose of the experiment was to measure the effect of data quality on decision-making efficiency. The advantage of this experiment was that such effects could be measured between and amongst treatment groups in a live setting.

The results of the research project show that accuracy as well as the amount of data can be deemed influencing factors on decision-making performance, whereas representational consistency of data has an effect on the time it takes to make a decision.

The research project may be most useful in the field of data quality management. It may also be profitable for creating information systems, and, in particular, for creating systems needed to support decision-making tasks. In addition to future research, the results of this project will also be a valuable resource for practical tasks in all kinds of industries. Without any doubt, there will be a broad and interested audience for the work Mr. Samitsch has accomplished through this research project.

Dr. Reinhard Bernsteiner

Profile of Management Center Innsbruck

Management Center Innsbruck (MCI) is an integral part of the unique "Comprehensive University Innsbruck" concept in Austria and has attained a leading position in international higher education as a result of its on-going quality and customer orientation. In the meantime 3,000 students, 1,000 faculty members, 200 partner universities worldwide and numerous graduates and employers appreciate the qualities of the Entrepreneurial School®.

MCI offers graduate, non-graduate and post-graduate educational programs of the highest standard to senior and junior managers from all management levels and branches. MCI's programs focus on all levels of the personality and include areas of state-of-the-art knowledge from science and practice relevant to business and society.

A wide range of Bachelor and Master study programs in the fields of management & society, technology & life sciences are offered. Curricula with a strong practical orientation, an international faculty and student body, the limited numbers of places, an optional semester abroad and internships with prestigious companies are among the many attractions of an MCI study program.

Embedded in a broad network of patrons, sponsors and partners, MCI is an important engine in the positioning of Innsbruck, Tyrol and Austria as a center for academic and international encounters. Our neighborly co-operation with the University of Innsbruck, the closeness to the lively Innsbruck Old Town and the powerful architecture of the location are an expression of the philosophy and the mission of this internationally exemplary higher education center.

www.mci.edu

Table of Contents

1 **Introduction** 1
  1.1 Objectives 2
  1.2 Overview of Master Thesis Process 2

2 **Literature Review** 4
  2.1 Data and Information Quality 4
    2.1.1 Intrinsic Data Quality 4
    2.1.2 Contextual Data Quality 5
    2.1.3 Representational Data Quality 6
    2.1.4 Accessibility Data Quality 6
  2.2 Research Areas of Data and Information Quality 8
    2.2.1 Impact of Data Quality on Organizational Performance 9
    2.2.2 Data Quality Issues in Health Care 11
    2.2.3 Assessing Data Quality 12
    2.2.4 Data Quality and Consumer Behavior 15
  2.3 Decision-Making in Decision Support Systems 16
    2.3.1 A Model of the Decision Making Process 17
    2.3.2 Decision Support Systems 18
    2.3.3 Presentation of data 20
    2.3.4 Accuracy of Data in Different Environments 20
    2.3.5 Decisions in the Mobile Environment 21
    2.3.6 The Knowledge-effort Tradeoff 22
  2.4 Summary of Factors Influencing Decision-Making Efficiency 23

3 **Research Question and Hypotheses** 25

4 **Methodology** 29
  4.1 Subjects of the Study 29
  4.2 Experimental Design 29
  4.3 Experimental Procedure 31
    4.3.1 Scenario and Tasks 32
    4.3.2 Independent Variables 35
    4.3.3 Dependent Variables 36
    4.3.4 Control Variables 36
    4.3.5 Treatment Groups 37

5 **Results** 39

6 **Discussion** 52
  6.1 Implications of the Study 52
  6.2 Data Quality Management 52

7	Conclusion	54
7.1	Limitations	54
7.2	Further Research	55
References		**57**

Note: The appendix is a separate document and can be retrieved online at www.springer.com referenced to author Christoph Samitsch.

List of Figures

Figure 1: Overall thesis approach 3
Figure 2: Data Quality Hierarchy – The four categories 7
Figure 3: Dependencies between data quality, organizational performance,
and enterprise systems success 10
Figure 4: Multidimensional Data Model for Analysis of Quality Measures 13
Figure 5: The General Heuristic Decision-making Procedure in the basic form 17
Figure 6: Google Maps as a Spatial Decision Support System 19
Figure 7: Potential factors impacting decision-making efficiency 23
Figure 8: Graphical representation of past demand data in the experiment 33
Figure 9: Data presented in tabular form 33
Figure 10: Age range distribution 39
Figure 11: Time comparisons between groups 40
Figure 12: Profit comparisons between groups 40
Figure 13: Comparing data quality dimension means between groups 41

Abstract

Data quality plays an important role in today's organizations, since poor quality of data can lead to poor decisions resulting in poor organizational productivity. Costs are then incurred by time spent on reversing what management has failed to accomplish. This study investigates the relationship between data quality and decision-making efficiency. It provides a guide for companies seeking to improve organizational performance by improving data quality, which is a combination of 16 different dimensions. Decision-making efficiency is composed of the time it takes to make a decision as well as decision-making performance. Another important aspect of the study is to find out whether there is a tradeoff between decision-making performance and the time for making a decision. Data was collected from an online experiment conducted with students at University of Nebraska Omaha and Management Center Innsbruck, as well as employees from an Omaha-based accounting and technology firm. 87 responses could be gathered. The experiment tested nine different data quality dimensions from the Information Quality Assessment Survey (IQAS). Participants were asked to make estimations based on information presented in various ways and formats. Results provide evidence that data accuracy and the amount of data have an effect on decision-making performance, while representational consistency has an effect on the time it takes to make a decision. No correlations could be found between decision-making performance and decision-making time. This suggests that subjects might be able to compensate poor data quality with their need for cognition as well as their level of self-efficacy. Further investigation in future research is therefore recommended.

Keywords: *Data quality, information quality, decision-making efficiency, decision-making process, decision support systems, assessing data quality*

1 Introduction

The demand for companies to convert raw data into information that supports decision-making is higher than ever before. Poor data quality often results in bad decision-making, which negatively impacts organizational performance. Forrester (2011) argues that *"there is movement toward investing and implementing data quality management technologies and best practices as the majority of companies believe their data quality management maturity is below average"*. Fisher et al. (2011: 4) summarize that poor data quality in organizations has a negative influence on productivity. The Data Warehousing Institute (TDWI) states that poor data quality costs businesses in the US $600 billion annually (Rockwell, 2012). Data quality is important to organizations in that it impacts customer satisfaction, operational costs, effectiveness of decision-making, and strategy creation and execution (Redman, 1998).

I see data and information quality as an essential part of management information systems – particularly the relationship between data quality and successful decision support systems. I believe that basing decisions on high quality data leads to improvements in organizational productivity. My main assumption is that data that is accurate, complete, up-to-date, and quickly aggregated will have a positive effect on decision-making efficiency. Furthermore, without being able to control the relationship between data quality and decision-making efficiency, companies may not be able to transition into a data-driven culture and, thus, increase organizational performance. I see great potential for improving data quality in organizations. Therefore, I think this Master thesis could serve as a basis for organizations seeking to develop strategies for improving data and information quality. Specifically, I want to examine how different levels of data and information quality affect the way in which people make decisions using decision support systems. This is significant as decision-making efficiency can have a direct impact on productivity. As an example, low decision-making efficiency due to poor data quality can influence measures such as DPMO (Defects per Million Opportunities). A study conducted by Forrester Consulting (2011) shows that operational processes and customer experience are most impacted by poor data quality. My motivation is to investigate the relationship between data quality and decision-making efficiency with the goal of providing a basis for improving organizational performance. Furthermore, with this study, I want to emphasize the importance of data quality and demonstrate that most poor decisions relate to poor data quality.

I see this Master thesis as an opportunity to develop something that is both valuable to me and to companies interested in making their data assets more valuable. In this Master thesis, I will first review existing literature and research in the field of data and information quality. I will describe decision support systems as a form of management information systems and discuss the dimensions of data quality in detail. Of specific importance is the Data Quality Hierarchy Model (Fisher et al., 2011: 43), which is fundamental in measuring data quality. I will then present my research questions and propose a methodology for gathering empirical data for achieving the objectives of this thesis. Finally, I will discuss my results and conclude with future research as well as limitations of this study.

1.1 Objectives

The main objective of this thesis is to investigate the relationship between data quality and decision-making efficiency. The assumption is that poor data quality has a negative effect on the time it takes to make a decision as well as decision-making performance. Conversely, data that is accurate, timely, understandable, and complete, might reduce the amount of time it takes to make decisions, independent of how well one can make a decision. In addition, it is possible that good data quality can increase performance, in that managers who can make decisions faster are more efficient. The goals of this study are as follows:

- To investigate how humans make decisions based on information presented in different ways.
- To find out whether humans are able to improve their decision-making abilities within a short period of time.
- To provide a basis for improving decision support systems.
- To provide recommendations on how to present data to better support good decision-making, especially for companies using business intelligence systems.
- To create new knowledge about data quality so that organizational performance can be improved.
- To find out how data quality can be improved.
- To find out what the most important dimensions of data quality are. This is of specific importance for the design of decision support systems, which will be one aspect of this study.

1.2 Overview of Master Thesis Process

For meeting the objectives of this Master's thesis, a process as outlined in the diagram below has been followed.

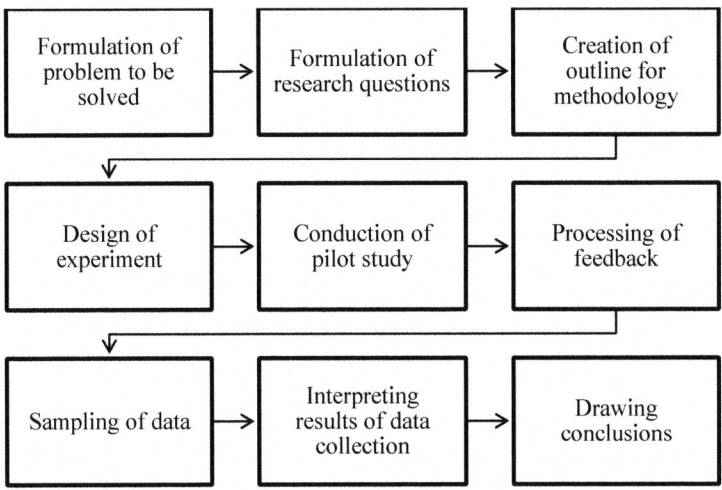

Figure 1: Overall thesis approach

The first step of the process was the discovery of a problem that has never been solved before. This was done by analyzing and exploring previous studies. From that, a research question was formulated and an experimental design was chosen as methodology for achieving the objectives of this thesis. After designing the experiment, a pilot study was conducted with the purpose of gaining early feedback. This feedback was used to improve the experiment and to remove inhibitors that can cause participants to cancel the experiment. 87 subjects were tested in the sampling phase while analysis of the collected data was being performed simultaneously to discover early indicators that would support the assumptions of this study. Finally, the results of the experiment were interpreted and a conclusion could be drawn. A review of existing literature was done during the whole duration of the thesis project.

2 Literature Review

In this chapter, definitions of data and information quality as well as decision support systems and the decision-making process will be presented. In addition, there will be an overview of research related to each of these topics. In particular, there are various factors that can influence one's decision-making efficiency. One main assumption of this study is that accuracy of information or how data is presented has a major impact on the time it takes to make a decision as well as decision-making performance. At the end of the chapter, a summary of factors that can have an effect on decision-making efficiency will be listed. These factors were extracted from existing literature.

2.1 Data and Information Quality

Understanding a user's decision-making processes is imperative for the data analyst to understand, since data quality is dependent on the business need. For example, one data consumer might rate data quality as very low because there is no sufficient amount of data available to make a decision. Another data consumer rates data quality as high, even though no sufficient data is available. In this case, other data quality dimensions might be important for this data consumer. Wang and Strong's Quality Framework, which comprises 16 different dimensions of data quality, clustered into four categories, demonstrates this (Fisher et al., 2011: 41-43), as outlined in the next four sections.

2.1.1 Intrinsic Data Quality

Fisher et al. (2011: 42-45) found a strong correlation between accuracy, believability, objectivity, and reputation of data. *"The high correlation indicates that the data consumers consider these four dimensions to be intrinsic in nature"*. The quality of the data is intrinsic when the quality of the data is directly knowable of the data. Batini & Scannapieco (2006: 20-21) emphasize that there are two kinds of data accuracy. One, syntactic accuracy considers the closeness of a value to a definition domain. In other words, a value v will be compared to a set of values D. If D contains v, then v is syntactically correct. For example, one might compare v = Jack with v' = John. Value v (Jack) would then be syntactically correct, even if v' = John, because Jack is a valid name in a list of persons' names. Two, there is semantic accuracy. This type of accuracy looks at how close a value v is to its true value v'. Semantic accuracy applies when there are relationships between sets of data. For example, one might consider a database with records about movies. For each movie title there is a director listed. If Peter Jackson was listed for The Lord of the Rings, then Peter Jackson would be considered semantically correct. If Peter Jackson was replaced by Quentin Tarantino, then Quentin Tarantino would be semantically incorrect. In both cases, the name of the director would be syntactically correct, since both of them exist in the domain of valid directors.

Wang & Strong (1996) noted that companies are focusing too much on accuracy as the only data quality dimension. The authors suggest considering a much broader conceptualization of data quality. In regards to believability of data, Fisher et al. (2011: 44) talk about multiple factors determining this dimension of data quality. One's knowledge, experience, and the degree of uncertainty in related data are known to be the influencing elements on believability. Furthermore, the authors suggest that believability might be much more important than accuracy because people are driven by their beliefs. The degree of judgment used in the data building process negatively correlates with how people perceive data to be objective. Finally, reputation of data might prevent people from considering how accurate data is. Reputation of data is built over time, and as Wang & Strong (1996) noted, both data and data sources can build reputation.

2.1.2 Contextual Data Quality

This category includes relevancy, completeness, value-added, timeliness, and amount of data (Fisher et al., 2011: 45). Wang & Strong (1996) brought up that the value-added dimension of data quality can be understood as data that adds value to a company's operations and, thus, gives the organization a competitive edge. Timeliness refers to how old data is. This is a very important attribute of data in manufacturing environments, as Fisher et al. (2011: 45) point out. Furthermore, some data are affected by age, whereas other data are not. As an example, the authors refer to George Washington, who was the first president of the United States. This information is unaffected by age. Incorrect decisions are often the result of financial decisions that are based on old data.

The quantity of information is a serious issue in evaluating data quality. A study on the use of graphs to aid decisions and a phenomenon called information overload was once conducted by Chan (2001). The scholar assumed that processing too much information can lead to making poor decisions. An experiment was conducted to show whether business managers would perform differently when treated with different loads of data. One group of subjects was given information with high load, whereas the other group of subjects was given information with nominal load. The results demonstrated that business managers under nominal information load could make higher quality decisions than those under high information load. This demonstrates that having more information is not necessarily better, or, in other words, does not necessarily lead to higher decision-making performance. The phenomenon of information overload could be proven in this study.

2.1.3 Representational Data Quality

This category reflects the importance of the presentation of data. It consists of the dimensions interpretability, ease of understanding, representational consistency, conciseness of representation, and manipulability. The category is *"based on the direct usability of data"* (Fisher et al., 2011: 47). Wang & Strong (1996) describe representational consistency as data that is continuously presented in the same format, consistently represented and formatted, as well as compatible with data that was presented previously. The scholars list clarity and readability as synonyms for the understandability of data. Attributes comprising the dimension of consistency are as follows: aesthetically pleasing, well-formatted, well-organized, and represented compactly. Fisher et al. (2011: 47) emphasize that there is a fine line between having troubles excerpting the essential point of an expression that is too long and having problems remembering what an acronym or short expression stands for when shortening long expressions. This could lead to errors in decision-making and, thus, it is suggested that data analysts work with users in determining the ideal version of data presentation. In addition, different users should be involved at different times.

2.1.4 Accessibility Data Quality

This category of data quality consists of the dimensions access and security. Questions to consider in this category are how and if data is available, and how well data is secured against unauthorized access. *"Accessibility and security are inversely related dimensions"*. As an example, time-consuming security features (e.g. login) that are added to restrict data access make it more difficult for users to get access to information they need for making decisions and, thus, lowers perceptions of data quality. Probably, increasing security decreases accessibility (Fisher et al., 2011: 47-48). Wang & Strong (1996) list the following attributes in connection to data access security: proprietary nature of data as well as inability of competitors to access data due to its restrictiveness.

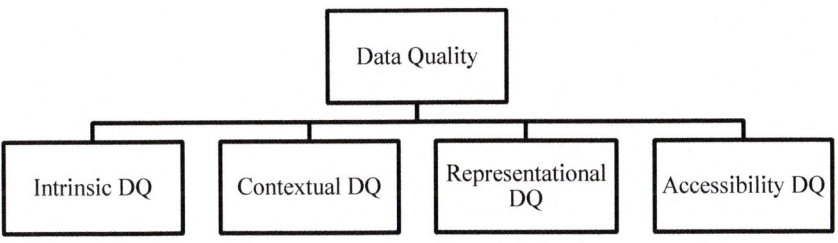

Figure 2: Data Quality Hierarchy – The four categories
Adapted from Fisher et al. (2011: 43)

Fisher et al. (2011: 44-48) illustrate some examples of different data quality dimensions. For instance, high data quality in terms of being accurate means that if there is an inventory database showing that 79 parts are in stock, then there should also be exactly the same amount of items in the stockroom. Another example is about the objectivity of data quality. The author states that *"users measure the quality of their data based on the degree of objectivity versus the degree of judgment used in creating it"*. Timeliness is referred to as how data is out-of-date. A strategic planner may perceive a data record as timely even if it is years old. The strategic planner might base their decisions on old information whereas a production manager might only value data that is within the hour. According to Sedera & Gable (2004), enterprise systems success is dependent upon attributes within the dimensions of system quality, information quality, individual impact, and organizational impact. In comparison to Wang & Strong's Quality Framework, which was illustrated before, Sedera & Gable present the following attributes for information quality: Availability, usability, understandability, relevance, format, and conciseness. Moreover, system accuracy is mentioned to belong to the category system quality. Decision effectiveness, learning, awareness and recall, as well as individual productivity are classified into individual impact.

The Canadian Institution for Health Care Information (2009: online) follows a data quality framework which consists of five different dimensions:
- Accuracy: Does information from a data holding coincide with real information?
- Timeliness: Is data still current when it is released?
- Comparability: Are all data holdings collecting data in a similar manner?
- Usability: Can data be easily accessed and understood by its users?
- Relevance: How does data meet a user's current potential future need?

The dimensions of the framework outlined before are part of an approach to *"systematically assess, document and improve data quality"* for all data holdings of the Canadian Institution of Health Care Information (2009: online). In this Master's thesis, Wang & Strong's (1996) data quality framework will be followed, since most research efforts have been undertaken into this direction.

Eppler & Muenzenmayer (2002) came up with a conceptual framework for information quality in the website context. They generally distinguish between content quality and media quality. For content quality, they further distinguish between relevant information and sound information. Attributes that can be associated with relevant information are as follows: comprehensive, accurate, clear, and applicable. Concise, consistent, correct, and current are attributes that make information sound. Media quality can be divided into the categories optimized process, with attributes like convenient, timely, traceable, and interactive, as well as reliable infrastructure, with attributes like accessible, secure, maintainable, and fast. Difficult navigation paths on a website are deemed an example of the convenience attribute.

2.2 Research Areas of Data and Information Quality

Batini & Scannapieco (2006: 16-17) talk about research areas that are being discussed in relation to data quality:

- Statistics: Making predictions and formulating decisions in different sets of contexts even if there is inaccurate data available is possible due to the development of a wide variety of methods and models in this field. Statistical methods help to measure and improve data quality.
- Knowledge representation: Rules and logical formulas are needed as the basis of a language that helps to represent knowledge. For improving data quality, reasoning about knowledge and the provision of a *"rich representation of the application domain"* are becoming more important.
- Data mining: This is the analytic process to find relationships among large sets of data. Exploratory data mining, which is defined *"as the preliminary process of discovering structure in a set of data using statistical summaries, visualization, and other means"*, can be used to improve data quality as well (Dasu & Johnson, 2003: 23).
- Management information systems: This research area is probably the most relevant for this Master's thesis. Data and knowledge in operational and decision business processes are resources that are gaining in value and importance.

- **Data integration:** Distributed, cooperative, and peer-to-peer information systems own heterogeneous data sources that need to be integrated so that a unified view of data can be provisioned.

Research studies that have been done in the fields mentioned above will be introduced in the following text.

2.2.1 Impact of Data Quality on Organizational Performance

Madnick et al. (2009) note that there are technical and nontechnical issues that may cause data and information quality problems:

"Organizations have increasingly invested in technology to collect, store, and process vast quantities of data. Even so, they often find themselves stymied in their efforts to translate this data into meaningful insights that they can use to improve business processes, make smart decisions, and create strategic advantages. Issues surrounding the quality of data and information that cause these difficulties range in nature from the technical (e.g., integration of data from disparate sources) to the nontechnical (e.g., lack of a cohesive strategy across an organization ensuring the right stakeholders have the right information in the right format at the right place and time)."

A literature review about previous research in data quality reveals that these technical and nontechnical issues have been frequently focused on by various scholars. Research of data and information quality is wide-reaching and affects many areas in the industry, as Tee et al. (2007) show in their article that can be found in the Accounting and Finance Journal. The scholars examined factors that influence the level of data quality in an organization. Senior managers as well as general users were sampled through interviews and surveys in a target organization. One key insight that is very relevant to this Master's thesis is that the perceptions of the relative importance of data quality dimensions were measured among and between senior managers and general users in this company. It turned out that there were no differences between the two groups across the three dimensions tested – accuracy, relevance, and timeliness. Accuracy was rated almost twice as important as the other two dimensions. In addition, management commitment and the presence of a champion for data quality both had a positive influence on the levels of data quality achieved in the target organization.

IBM's white paper talks about solving data quality issues through improved data quality management. Retail and manufacturing businesses constantly expand their channels for reaching customers. With increasing global economic complexity, maintaining high levels of data quality becomes a problem. In the production industry, it is important to maintain high levels of data quality as a means of reducing waste in the supply chain (IBM, 2010).

An intensive literature review about impacts of factors on the success of information systems was done by Petter, DeLone & McLean (2008). The scholars point out that there are six major dimensions that are known to have an influence on the successful usage of information systems: system quality, information quality, service quality, use, user satisfaction, and net benefits. In comparison, many of the attributes within these six dimensions are very similar to the attributes that can be found in Wang & Strong's (1996) framework of data quality dimensions. For example, understandability and user friendliness of a system are two attributes of system quality. These might be closely related to ease of understanding as well as interpretability of data in Wang & Strong's framework.

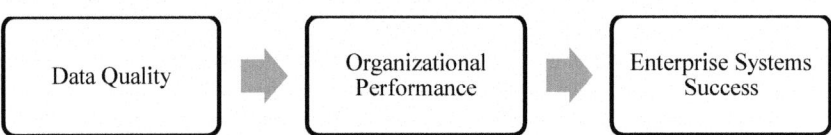

Figure 3: Dependencies between data quality, organizational performance, and enterprise systems success

The figure above demonstrates the importance of data quality. Considering previous research on dependencies between data quality dimensions, information systems success, and organizational performance, a big picture can be drawn. Sedera & Gable (2004) argued that overall productivity of an organization has an impact on the success of enterprise systems, whereas Fisher et al. (2011: 4) summarize that data quality in organizations has an influence on productivity.

In a distributed project setting, the quality of aggregate project-status data that needs to be sent between organizations can be a major problem in a lot of companies. Managers must make sourcing decisions in distributed software projects based on data that are flawed, even though the data are inaccurate. Most of the erroneous data is mainly caused by *"exchanging data across multiple systems, combining data from multiple sources, and from legacy applications"*. Furthermore, collecting project-status data in a timely manner is often an issue. The importance of timeliness as a data quality dimension which is correlating with accuracy suggests that project-status data should be updated in a real-time manner. Performance is also negatively influenced by inaccurate data. One approach for improving data quality in distributed project settings is to apply a Kalman-Bucy filter to present more accurate data to managers who need to make sourcing decisions (Joglekar, Anderson & Shankaranarayanan, 2013).

Xu et al. (2002) report improved information quality as one of the benefits of implementing ERP systems, whereas Cao & Zhu (2013) view it from a different perspective and talk about data quality problems in ERP-enabled manufacturing.

Changes in the Bill of Materials (BOM) require adjustments in calculating materials required, and in generating product, purchase, as well as work orders. The scholars found that adjustments of these data were especially difficult if the Bill of Materials had to be changed frequently. Inaccurate data in processes such as production planning, logistics, or manufacturing would be the result of these frequent changes. It was also found that are two characteristics of ERP systems that are very hard to extinguish, but they can cause data quality problems: 1) Complex interactions of components, and 2) tight coupling due to the implantation of an ERP system.

Furthermore, inconsistencies and inaccuracies in data sets can pollute a data source. This might cause difficulties in performing data analysis. For transactional systems, it means that orders taken incorrectly, or errors occurring in packaging, documentation, or billing, can cause dissatisfied customers, or can result in additional material and labor costs. In a case study that involved the implementation of an ERP system, it was found that a cross-departmental increase in ERP system usage had increased overall data accuracy in the company (Vosburg & Kumar, 2001).

In general, data inaccuracies in sets of data seem to be a crucial issue in companies. Moreover, it seems as if manufacturing firms and organizations that are utilizing ERP systems need to be very aware of data quality issues. In the next subsections, light will be shed on data quality issues in the health care industry, as well as options for assessing data quality. Knowledge about how to measure data quality will be needed in this study so that possible impacts on decision-making efficiency can be determined.

2.2.2 Data Quality Issues in Health Care

According to McNaull et al. (2012), assisted living technologies use artificial intelligence and automated reasoning to understand the behavior of people who need care due to chronic diseases, and people who need health and social care provision due to their age. Inherently, ambient intelligence-based systems, or Ambient Assisted Living (AAL) technologies make it possible for people to extend the time they live at home by providing feedback to users and carrying out particular actions based on patterns that these systems are able to observe. There are certain data quality issues that may cause these systems to provide assistance based on inaccurate data and, thus, the person using such a system may be detrimentally affected. It is essential that information in these systems is sent and received in a timely manner as events are happening. Moreover, poor data quality can lead to poor information quality, which furthermore is closely linked to poor-quality contextual knowledge. The authors of this paper suggest a model to implement quality-control measures into Ambient Assisted Living systems. The way it works is to feedback knowledge gained during the system's reasoning cycle and using it for conducting further data quality checks.

Curé (2012) emphasizes the importance of high data quality in drug databases which are often exploited by health care systems and services. Poor data quality, e.g. the inaccuracy of drug contraindications, can have a severe negative impact on a patient's health condition. The author notes that data quality should be ensured in terms of data completeness and soundness. In his study, Olivier Curé presents special technologies to represent hierarchical structures of pharmacology information (e.g. the technology of the Semantic Web). Moreover, SPARQL is presented in the article as a query language for resolving issues of conditional dependencies (CINDs – conditional inclusion dependencies) for these graph-oriented structures. In Curé's study, an experiment was conducted in which CINDs in a drug database with both real and synthetic datasets were investigated. The author describes attempts to improve data quality in this drug database.

2.2.3 Assessing Data Quality

Pipino, Lee & Wang (2002) tried to answer the question of how good a company's data quality is. The authors describe principles to develop data quality metrics that are useful for measuring data quality. The core of their study was the presentation of three functional forms for developing objective data quality metrics. As an example, the Simple Ratio *"measures the ratio of desired outcomes to total outcomes"*, subtracted from 1.

Embury et al. (2009) talk about variability of data quality in query-able data repositories. Data with low quality can be useful, but only if data consumers are aware of the data quality problems. Quality measures computed by the information provided have been used to incorporate quality constraints into database queries. The authors describe the possibility of embedding data quality constraints into a query. These constraints should describe the consumer's data quality requirements. The problem that the research team attempted to address was that poor data quality is a consequence of information providers who define quality constraints. Their idea was to increase the level of data quality by incorporating quality constraints into database queries whereas users define quality such that domain-specific notions of quality can be embedded.

Heinrich & Klier (2011) propose a novel method for assessing data currency (one dimension of data quality, as mentioned earlier). Data currency is an important aspect of data quality management. In terms of quality in information systems, the authors distinguish between quality of design and quality of conformance. The latter is essential for this study, since it refers to *"the degree of correspondence between the data values stored in a database and the corresponding real world counterparts"*. As an example, data values stored in the database might not be up-to-date and, thus, lack quality of conformance. In other words, these data sets do not correspond with their real world counterparts.

Berti-Équille et al. (2011) propose a novel approach for measuring and investigating information quality. The scholars developed a model which can be transversally applied by users, designers, and developers. In their study, the quality of customer information at a French electricity company and patient records at a French medial institute were analyzed to create a multidimensional notion of multidimensional information exploration. Measures of data quality were stored in a star-like database. Quality dimensions (e.g. accuracy, response time, readability) are complimentary to analysis dimensions, which are analysis criteria such as date of data quality assessment, quality goals, and actors involved in the assessment. The model uses a GQM paradigm, which stands for "Goal-Question-Measure". Applied to the multidimensional model of data quality, goals are set at a conceptual level (e.g. *"reduce the number of returns in customer mails"*), questions are asked at an operational level (e.g. *"which is the amount of syntactic errors in customer addresses?"*), and measures are defined for the quantitative level to quantify answers to questions (e.g. *"the percentage of data satisfying a syntax rule"*). A method, or a set of measurement methods to compute the measures are included in the model as well. Indicators as well as analysis criteria are included in the multidimensional data model for analysis of quality measures. A brief description of the indicators and analysis criteria is presented after the graph.

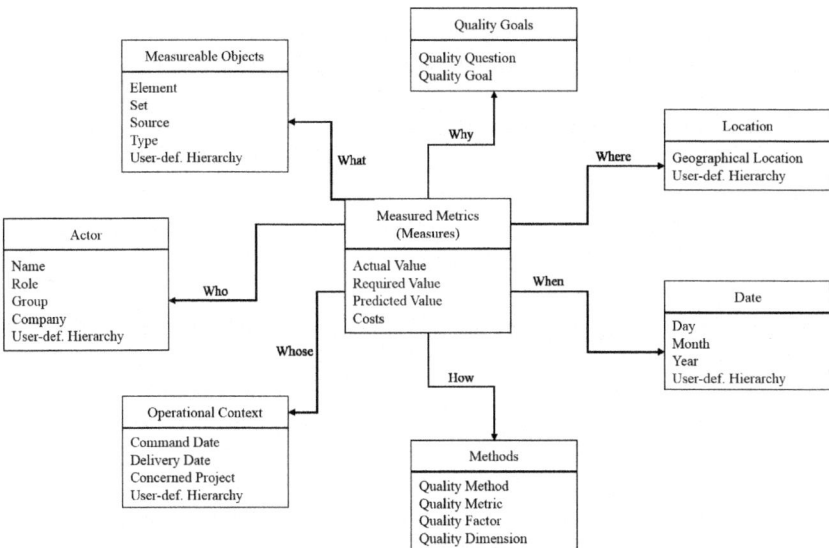

Figure 4: Multidimensional Data Model for Analysis of Quality Measures
Adapted from Berti-Équille (2011)

Analysis criteria included in the model (Berti-Équille, 2011):
- Date: This criterion includes the date on which the quality measure was recorded, in the typical day-month-year structure.
- Measurable objects: The type of object as well as the object examined for calculating data quality is indicated in this dimension. The object can be a data record in a database.
- Quality methods: This dimension refers to how the quality measures were recorded.
- Quality goals: The purpose of recording the quality measure is reflected in this section of the model.
- Location: Measures are associated to geographical locations. As an example, data about electricity consumption of a household can be associated to the location of the household.
- Actor: This section of the model indicates the person who took the quality measurement. Actors can also be enterprises or groups of people.
- Operational context: A quality problem is associated with a business problem from which it originates. Linked to it are the date of request, the deliverable data, the sponsor, and the operational constraints.

Here are the indicators that this multidimensional model contains (Berti-Équille, 2011):
- Actual quality value: This is the quality measure that was calculated by the measurement method.
- Required quality value: This is defined by the determination of a quality goal. The bounds within which the value is required to be are indicated in this metric.
- Predicted quality value: This value can either originate from a benchmark or from users' expectations about what they think the quality value might be.
- Non-quality cost: Those are the costs that emanate from poor quality objects that were assumed by the company.

The indent of this model is to support the exploration of the relationships between quality metrics, quality factors, and quality dimensions, and to derive quality requirements from business requirements by involving users, designers, and developers. An instance of the model has been put into practice at a medial institution in France. Moreover, the model is a step towards *"measuring and exploring the complex notion of quality in a holistic way"* (Berti-Équille, 2011).

How data quality in the web context can be measured, was demonstrated by Eppler & Muenzenmayer (2002). They list five types of tools that can be used for this purpose:

- Performance monitoring: Speed and reliability are deemed attributes of data quality in the web context that can be measured with tools that help monitor availability and performance of servers.
- Site analyzer: This is software that is available for checking whether a website has broken links and anchors, or whether there are any failures in a web form. Tools like these are also capable of examining browser compatibility or the site inventory including used image maps or types of documents. Site analyzers mainly focus on the website as a product, but not on user behavior.
- Traffic analyzer: Page hits, view, and visits as well as standard reports that investigate search engine, keywords, or search phrases used, can be considered standard functionality of these types of tools.
- Web mining: These are tools to integrate data from tools like traffic analyzers or website analyzers as well as legacy systems.
- User feedback: Many data quality dimensions in the web context cannot be measured technically. Therefore, user feedback helps to get insight into dimensions like comprehensiveness, clarity, and accuracy of data. User feedback can typically be gained from polls or interviews.

2.2.4 Data Quality and Consumer Behavior

When consumers make decisions (e.g. purchase decisions), they compensate information that is incomplete and erroneous by a correspondence of confidence and accuracy, called calibration. Accuracy is about what we know, and confidence *"reflects what we think we know"*. As an example, poor calibration of a consumer's knowledge would be if the person is very confident that he or she has found the lowest price for a certain product in a specific store, but he or she finds out that the same item is offered for a lower price at stores that he/she subsequently goes to. In contrast, good calibration would be if the consumer found out that the subsequent stores offered the same item for a higher price. In decision-making processes, 100% accuracy equates to the right answer, whereas being 100% confident that it might be the right answer is not necessarily correlated to the accuracy of the decision. Research has found out that when consumers rely on information from their past memories, they will be less accurate in making a decision. This suggests that their overconfidence in these situations does not correlate with accuracy of making a decision. Conversely, when consumers feel that they are making a guess, they are mostly under-confident because they are relying on their intuition. It has also been shown that lower self-esteem leads to a reduction in "miscalibration" – the difference between accuracy and confidence (Alba & Hutchinson, 2000). One main assumption of this Master's thesis is that humans are able to compensate incomplete information by their confidence and ability to make predictions without considering the quality of data. The focus of this research will be on how accurate humans are in making decisions while being influenced by different levels of data quality. Incomplete data is one of the data quality dimensions.

Missing information can have effects on purchase evaluations. There is evidence in literature that individuals average values of product attributes when assessing alternatives. Satisfaction ratings of a purchase that was made by a customer decrease when the number of attributes with missing information (e.g. price tag without price) increases. Information that is missing for one attribute of a product can lead to a decrease in how the present attributes affect consumer evaluation. For this to happen, two attributes have to be negatively related. If they are positively related, the presentation of an attribute that holds intermediate information does not differ from the presentation of an attribute without any information presented. Consumers form evaluations based on both information that they have and information they do not have. This means that values for missing information are imputed by consumers. This furthermore has an effect on the value that is formed for available information (Richard & Irwin, 1985).

Similarly, presented information is affected by missing information. Past research suggests that consumers who note missing attributes of product descriptions either try to find more information about the product or they deduce the value of information that is missing on an attribute. The scholars were able to explain this behavior by developing an inference model that demonstrates correlations between product attributes. For example, there is a negative correlation between capacity and energy cost for refrigerators. If information on energy cost is missing for a product, it will lead to discounting, which is a consumer-rating that is less positive than it would be if the information was there. This only applies to negatively correlated product attributes (Simmons & Lynch, 1991).

2.3 Decision-Making in Decision Support Systems

This section starts with a definition of decision support systems as well as decision-making. An overview of the general model of the decision-making process is given. Furthermore, previous research related to factors influencing decision-making as well as relevant research regarding decision support systems will be provided. An emphasis will be put on factors influencing decision-making efficiency (time and performance). At the end of the chapter, there will be a brief summary of factors that were found to impact decision makers in their decision-making process.

2.3.1 A Model of the Decision Making Process

Sugumaran & DeGroote (2011, 2-3) define decision as *"a choice that is made between two or more alternatives"*. Furthermore, the authors state that minimum objectives and/or more demanding objectives are preceding the step of forming potential choices. Lunenburg (2010) talks about three key components in the decision-making process. One, a choice has to be made from a certain amount of options. Two, knowledge about how the decision was made has to be gained. Three, in order to get to a final decision, there has to be a purpose or target involved in the decision-making process. Grünig & Kühn (2005: 7-8) note that there are numerous ways a decision can be approached. One option is to use one's intuition. However, the problem will not be carefully reflected then. Another way is adhering to routine procedures that are already known to the decision maker(s). Decisions can also be made by adopting what experts suggested without questioning their opinion. The fourth approach is choosing an alternative randomly. Finally, information can be used as a basis to make a decision.

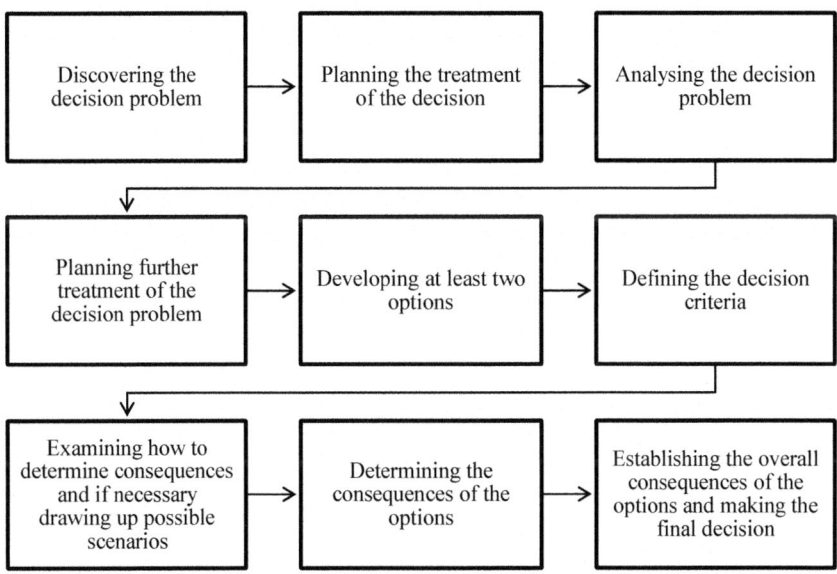

Figure 5: The General Heuristic Decision-making Procedure in the basic form
Adapted from Grünig & Kühn (2005: 66)

In this Master's thesis, the focus is on how decision-making efficiency changes due to different levels of data quality. One main aspect of it is the analysis of data as one possible decision-making approach versus using one's intuition (as outlined before). It is important to review the process of how humans naturally make decisions. The experiment conducted for this study (as described later) was built on an understanding and analysis of the decision-making process. Grünig & Kühn (2005: 65-75) proposed a sequence of steps in the decision-making process which they named the general heuristic decision-making procedure. They distinguish between a basic and a more complex form of the procedure. In this study, the simple version of the procedure was chosen to build the experiment on. The reason is that insight has to be created first before one can move on to the complex version of the process.

The general heuristic decision-making process is repeated until the decision maker has found a solution that is acceptable to solve the decision-making problem discovered in the first step. It is necessary to repeat steps five to nine if the options assessed in the process have not resulted in satisfaction (Grünig & Kühn, 2005: 65). Similar to Grünig & Kühn's model, Raghunathan (1999) views the decision-making process as an input-process-output model. Decision makers produce decisions based on information that are provided to them by IT systems. This information is considered inputs of this model. The decisions made are considered outputs.

Sugumaran & DeGrotte (2011: 8-9) present a general process for making spatial decisions. The process is very similar to the aforementioned decision process as developed by Grünig & Kühn. It involves the following steps: 1) problem definition, 2) setting goals and objectives, 3) finding potential decision alternatives, 4) evaluating the alternatives found, 5) selecting the final alternative chosen, and finally, 6) implementing the alternative. The steps are not necessarily linear. One can go back from one phase to another. For example, new knowledge might be generated or one can have new ideas and, thus, can return to a previous step in the process.

2.3.2 Decision Support Systems

Decision support systems *"focus on support or automation of decision making in organizations"*. Inputs of a decision support system can be data, information, and knowledge, whereas data can come from sources like data warehouses and operational systems. A decision recommendation is the output of such a system. Information technologies are the components that make a decision support system (Sabherwal & Becerra-Fernandez, 2011: 11-12). Decision support systems are a special form of a management information system. A main element of such a system is to provide information to managers in a format that is usable to them. Furthermore, a decision support system encompasses three key components: 1) a comprehensive, integrated database, 2) the mathematical models, and 3) the ad hoc inquiry facilities. Moreover, data quality plays an important role for decision support systems to be efficient and effective to management (Fisher et al., 2012: 53).

Decision support systems aid the user by integrating database management systems with modeling and analysis as well as providing user interfaces for interacting with the user. Simply put, decision support systems include the usage of computers to aid decisions. In spatial decision-making processes, users can benefit greatly from decision support systems. It is estimated that 80% of data that managers are using to make decisions are geographically related. Complex information needs to be processed in spatial decision-making processes. Tools like MapQuest or Google Maps are modern decision support systems and support users in making routing decisions (Sugumaran & DeGroote, 2011: 3-12).

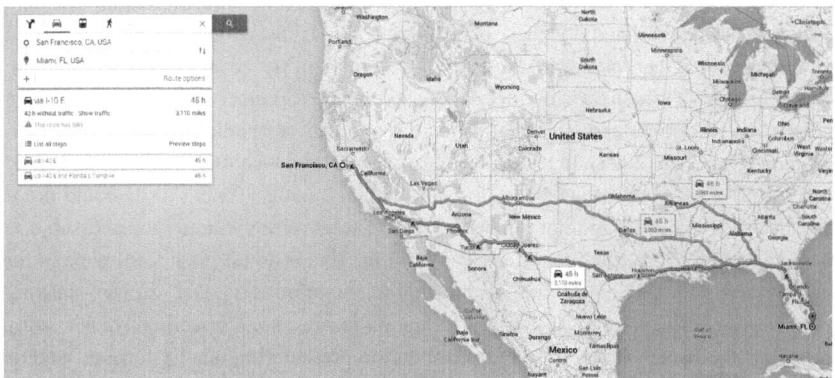

Figure 6: Google Maps as a Spatial Decision Support System

In the figure above, Google Maps is illustrated as an example of a spatial decision support system. According to Sugumaran & DeGroote (2011: 14), spatial decision support systems are

> *"integrated computer systems that support decision makers in addressing semistructured or unstructured spatial problems in an interactive and iterative way with functionality for handling spatial and nonspatial databases, analytical modeling capabilities, decision support utilities such as scenario analysis, and effective data and information presentation utilities".*

2.3.3 Presentation of data

Research on decision support systems and decision making has been done in different areas of the industry. Among others, supply chain management and logistics has been a focus for improving data quality in order to improve decision-making tasks. General research efforts have been undertaken on how decision making is influenced by data that is presented in different ways.

Depending on graphical representation of data, decision makers will perform differently on information acquisition tasks. Research has shown that the dimensions time and accuracy of performance are positively affected when information is presented in graphs instead of tables, even if graphs contain the same information. In fact, if information is presented by using both graphs and tables at the same time, performance involving information gathering activities increases. This can possibly be explained by the paradigm of cognitive fit, which suggests that problem representation and the problem solving task are related to each other in a way as they both affect the mental representation of a problem and, thus, will have a final influence on the problem solution (Vessey, 1991). Whether or not decision markers' performance is increased by using graphs instead of tabular presentation of data under information overload was also examined by Chan (2001). In contrast to Vessey (1991) who showed evidence that using graphs has a positive influence on decision-making quality, Chan (2001) could proof that decision quality is similar between subjects who were given graphs and subjects who information was presented to in tabular form. This is an essential starting point for this Master's thesis, since one of the main assumptions is that decision-making efficiency is influenced by the way information is presented. Specifically, this study considers the usage of graphs versus information presented in tabular form as well as information presented using both graphs and tables. Considering Chan's and Vessey's research efforts, there may also be other factors that impact human decision-making efficiency. This might be an explanation for the different results of the studies mentioned before.

2.3.4 Accuracy of Data in Different Environments

Other research has investigated factors influencing actual decision quality versus perceived decision-making quality. A major insight that was developed is that information quality has no influence on the actual decision-making quality if the decision problem is perfectly non-deterministic. On the contrary, if the decision problem is perfectly deterministic, information quality has a positive influence on decision-making quality. In both environments, the decision-maker quality, which refers to quality of the decision-making process, is positively related to the expected decision quality. A conclusion that can be drawn from these results is that higher information quality in IT systems leads to higher organizational performance (Raghunathan, 1999). In his research, Raghunathan performed tests on the accuracy dimension as part of the data quality framework which encompasses multiple data quality dimensions. Furthermore, he suggested extending his study with more data quality dimensions. Accuracy of data can affect a whole supply chain, as discussed by the author of the study paper.

Imprecision of demand information is one of the challenges in using and setting up a decision support system in logistic processes. Demand information provided along the supply chain has to be credible in order for safety stock costs and backorder to be minimized. Using Vendor Management Inventory (VMI) as a decision support system to evenly distribute inventory status and demand information throughout the whole supply chain is recommended, since the ordering process is influenced by the quality of demand information (Kristiano et al, 2012).

In their study about judgmental forecasting with interactive forecasting support systems, Lim & O'Connor (1996) found that, when forecasting tasks with using interactive decision support systems, people tend to select information that is less reliable instead of acquiring enough information for aggregating data such that they can make better decisions. The reason for this might be that people might find it difficult aggregating pieces of information so that it is more beneficial to them. Instead, they would rather use the information they already have.

2.3.5 Decisions in the Mobile Environment

Cowie & Burstein (2007) argue that decisions being made in a mobile environment are dynamic. Their proposition is that measures of Quality of the Data (QoD) in mobile decision support systems can be used to benefit a mobile decision maker. The scholars developed a model to demonstrate parameters that have an effect on data quality on mobile devices. These parameters can be clustered into three main categories:

- Technology-related parameters: An aggregation of the measures energy, security, connectivity, etc. is one whole context in which data quality can be represented.
- User-related parameters: The authors distinguish between stability of scores and stability of weights. Scores can be static or dynamic. As an example, company reputation would be considered static, since it does not change from one minute to the other. Dividend yield can be considered dynamic due to its frequent changes. Quality of data for mobile users is higher when the stability of scores is displayed to them. For instance, 0 could reflect a dynamic value that changes from one second to the other, whereas 100 could indicate the most static value.

...lated parameters: These include measures such as completeness, ...nd accuracy, whereas completeness and currency can be calculated. ...ple, currency is based on frequency of updates and current time.

2.3. Knowledge-effort Tradeoff

In theory, for *"a given level of effort, users with greater knowledge will achieve greater accuracy"*, and, similarly, *"for a given level of knowledge, users who exert greater effort will achieve greater accuracy"*. System restrictiveness in decision support systems has been proven to have an effect on how knowledge, effort, and accuracy are interrelated. For this purpose, two decision support systems with different levels of restrictiveness were developed by Davern & Kamis (2010):

- ELIM (eliminative tool): This decision support system is relatively restrictive, meaning that fewer decision strategies are provided.
- PS (parametric search tool): This tool is less restrictive than the eliminative tool. The range of processes that are supported by it is greater. In other words, the amount of decision strategies that are provided is higher than for the ELIM system.

An experimental study in which subjects were tested on both of these systems revealed that knowledge negatively affects performance in less restrictive decision support systems, even though greater performance returns can be achieved by increasing efforts. One of the explanations of this negative correlation between knowledge and performance was that subjects with greater knowledge might not display as much care or effort. Another reason could be that there is a worse cognitive fit of exercising decision-making strategies used by more knowledgeable people. This again raises the issue of the impact of the design of decision tools on performance (Davern & Kamis, 2010). Vessey (1991) was able to uncover a similar finding, as mentioned earlier. The effect of the presentation of data on decision making performance is a crucial part of this research and will be further examined by applying an experimental design method. Davern & Kamis (2010) suggest further research on this.

Kuo et al. (2004) conducted a study to explore the tradeoff between effort and accuracy when using different search strategies on the web. Similarly to Davern & Kamis's study, the authors built their assumptions on the underlying principle of the effort-accuracy tradeoff model. In addition, Social Cognitive Theory (SCT) could explain how one's level of self-efficacy is a factor that has an impact on web search behavior. Self-efficacy, which is one's capability to accomplish tasks and achieve goals, plays an important role in finding accurate information. More specifically, subjects with higher self-efficacy do not need additional web search time (effort to find information) in order to achieve a higher level of accuracy in the information they find. Furthermore, the difference between individuals with low self-efficacy and high self-efficacy is that high self-efficacy leads to subjects spending less time (effort) on information gathering and decision-making tasks, but still the same level of accuracy can be achieved. Research has shown that people tend to use a strategy that they have adopted from experience when solving problems in a particular problem domain. Experience was a factor that has been investigated by the authors of this research study. Specifically, they wanted to find out how one's experience with web search strategies influences the effort-accuracy tradeoff on search decisions that individuals are making when searching the web. The finding was that users do not change their effort level in various situations when they are experienced, and when they show a high level of self-efficacy.

2.4 Summary of Factors Influencing Decision-Making Efficiency

A range of factors impacting decision-making efficiency could be identified by reviewing existing literature. In fact, decision-making efficiency might be most influenced by data quality – as literature suggest. Additionally, knowledge about a domain, the restrictiveness and the design of a decision tool are factors considered having an influence on how well decision makers perform when they base their decisions on information that is presented to them. Most research has been done on data accuracy. Secondary emphasis has been put on timeliness and completeness of data. It appears as if data quality has a major impact on the outcome of a decision, whereas one's ability to make accurate predictions may only be a helpful skill in some cases. One's level of self-efficacy and experience might be additional factors that could have an effect on how data quality is perceived as well as on how well someone performs on decision-making tasks (see section before).

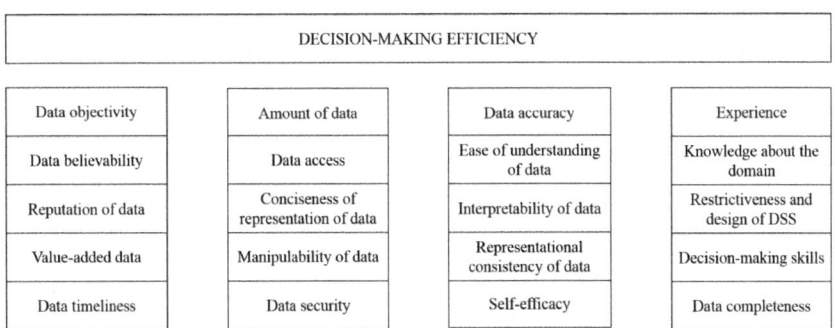

Figure 7: Potential factors impacting decision-making efficiency

In this Master's thesis, nine out of sixteen data quality dimensions will be included in an online experiment, which will be explained later in this paper. As illustrated in the graph above, there could be many factors directly affecting decision-making efficiency. There might also be some others which are not shown in the graph. Finding these hidden factors that could not be discovered by previous studies would be a topic for future research.

3 Research Question and Hypotheses

The main focus of this Master' thesis is to investigate the relationship between nine dimensions of data quality and decision-making efficiency measures such as time and one's ability to make predictions. The reason why exactly nine dimensions were chosen is explained later in the paper. The first research question can be defined as follows.

> RQ1: *Can variations in decision-making efficiency be explained in terms of variations in data quality dimensions?*

Hypotheses for RQ1

H_1: The variables accuracy, timeliness, completeness, appropriate amount, interpretability, ease of understanding, representational consistency, concise representation, and relevancy have no influence on the time it takes to make a decision.

H_2: The variables accuracy, timeliness, completeness, appropriate amount, interpretability, ease of understanding, representational consistency, concise representation, and relevancy of information have no influence on decision-making performance.

As outlined above, hypothesis H_1 aims at the investigation of the variable time (for making a decision), H_2 aims at the investigation of the variable decision-making performance.

Furthermore, demographic variables like gender, age, and variables such as supporting tools used to perform the experiment were included in the research in order to test whether there are additional factors on top of data quality that might impact the results. As an example, women and men might differ in regards to their ability to predict future happenings. Another example could be that there is a difference in terms of the amount of time it takes to make a decision between people whose primary occupation is student, and people whose primary occupation is something else. Thus, the second research question can be formulated as presented below.

> RQ2: *Can variations in decision-making efficiency be explained in terms of variations in data quality dimensions, age, occupation, gender, and supporting tools used to perform decision-making tasks?*

Hypotheses for RQ2

H_3: The variables accuracy, timeliness, completeness, appropriate amount, interpretability, ease of understanding, representational consistency, concise representation, relevancy, age, occupation, and supporting tools used have no influence on the time it takes to make a decision.

H_4: The variables accuracy, timeliness, completeness, appropriate amount, interpretability, ease of understanding, representational consistency, concise representation, relevancy, age, occupation, and supporting tools used of information have no influence on decision-making performance.

Another assumption of the study is that making a decision will have a learning effect on making a similar decision at a later time. Applied to the dimensions of data quality, a poor decision made due to poor data quality might improve one's decision-making abilities in a similar situation in the future. Hence, the third research question for this study is as follows.

RQ3: How does decision-making efficiency change when similar tasks have to be performed subsequently?

For research question number three, the learnability rate is important to consider. Specifically, time and ability to make predictions about the future will be measured for each decision to be made in the experiment, which will be described in detail in the upcoming chapter. Research question three was evaluated by viewing the experiment as three tasks participants needed to complete, whereas one task relates to one estimation. Each estimation is considered a group. The groups can then be compared against each other in terms of decision-making performance.

Hypotheses for RQ3

H_5: μ decision-making performance for task one = μ decision-making performance task two.

H_6: μ decision-making performance for task two = μ decision-making performance task three.

This research also aims at investigating whether time has a positive influence on decision-making performance. Kuo et al. (2004) have already found out that there might be a tradeoff between effort and decision-making accuracy, whereas effort relates to time.

RQ4: *What is the tradeoff between the amount of time it takes to make a decision and decision-making performance?*

This research question can be tested in two ways. One way is to check whether a linear relationship between decision-making performance and decision-making time exists. The other way is to assume that decision-making performance is dependent on time. Another purpose of this research question is to see if the relationships between these two variables are negative or positive.

Hypotheses for RQ4

H_7: There is no linear relationship between decision-making performance and the time it takes to make a decision for the overall scenario.

H_8: There is no linear relationship between decision-making performance and the time it takes to make a decision for task one.

H_9: There is no linear relationship between decision-making performance and the time it takes to make a decision for task two.

H_{10}: There is no linear relationship between decision-making performance and the time it takes to make a decision for task three.

Research question number four aims at Davern & Kamis's (2010) study. The knowledge-effort tradeoff will be examined by measuring both time and decision-making performance, as discussed in the results section of this paper.

For this research, it is important to consider that there might be variables which could cause a change in perceived data quality levels. As an example, male participants may perceive data and information quality differently than female participants. In order to find out such relationships, one can formulate another research question.

RQ5: *How does age, gender, supporting tools used for making decisions, and occupation influence perceptions of data quality?*

Hypotheses for RQ5

H_{11}: µ perceived data quality males = µ perceived data quality females.

H_{12}: µ perceived data quality students = µ perceived data quality non-students.

H_{13}: Data quality is perceived the same across six different age groups.

H_{14}: There is no relationship between using a calculator for supporting estimations and perceived data quality.

H_{15}: There is no relationship between using paper and pen for supporting estimations and perceived data quality.

Finally, a major contribution of this thesis will be the validation of the Information Quality Assessment Survey (IQAS) for finding out whether there are any items that can be eliminated from the questionnaire, which is a major part of the experiment. This will be explained in detail in the results section of the paper.

4 Methodology

In this chapter, the methodological approach to conduct this research study is explained in detail. The nature of this research project is quantitative. An experimental design was chosen to collect research data from the subjects. The chapter starts with a description of the participants and how they were recruited. Second, an explanation will be given about why an experimental design was chosen to collect empirical data from subjects, and how the experiment was conducted. Items were taken from the Information Quality Assessment Survey and adapted for this thesis so that data quality could be assessed. Only items related to measureable quality dimensions were picked. Third, independent, dependent, and control variables involved in this research study are listed and explained in this section. A decision support system was designed to serve as the basis for the conducted experiment. Tasks given to participants are described in this chapter and, finally, the procedure of how the experiment was performed will be outlined.

4.1 Subjects of the Study

Primarily, students at University of Nebraska Omaha and Management Center Innsbruck were chosen to participate in the experiment, which was entirely held online. In addition, employees from an accounting and technology firm in Omaha, Nebraska, were recruited, with the purpose to make comparisons between two groups: 1) subjects who primarily consider themselves students, and 2) subjects whose primary occupation is other than student. Students at University of Nebraska Omaha were recruited through professors who acted as the liaison between the primary investigator of this study and their students. Professors were contacted and asked if they would be interested having their students to participate in a research study. An explanation of the nature of the study, together with a link to the online experiment, was then sent to the interested parties, who, for the most part, were provided a computer lab during class to participate in the study. The entire experiment was hosted online in order to provide a more flexible interaction with subjects as well as to standardize the data collection process. For students of Management Center Innsbruck, the link to the online experiment was posted on a learning management system that is accessible to them. The link was also posted on Facebook as an additional source for responses.

4.2 Experimental Design

In the present study, an experimental design was used to explore the relationship between a chosen set of data quality dimensions and decision-making efficiency by collecting data from participants. The experiment was conducted online. The idea behind that was to have more flexibility (e.g. to reach subjects located outside the near research area).

According to Crano & Brewer (2002: 146), experimental research involves *"systematically controlling the variation in the independent variable (or variables) to assess its causal impact"*. Relating to this research study, variations of data quality were created so that the causal impact on decision-making efficiency could be assessed. For the experiment, participants were not randomly recruited, but they were randomly assigned into five different treatment groups. Therefore, a true experiment has not been conducted, but rather, a quasi-experimental design was used to pursue the objectives of this research study. Crano & Brewer (2002: 151) mention that quasi-experimental designs are very similar to true experiments, but with the difference that a random assignment of the sample is absent.

In terms of the type of the experiment, the study follows the structure of a comparative design. David & Sutton (2004: 136) explain that a comparative design should be chosen when similarities and differences between certain groups are the main focus of the research effort. Moreover, the authors discuss the ethics of conducting quantitative research (2004: 126-137):

- Confidentiality and anonymity: It is suggested that participants should be contacted by the research team. In some cases, this might be difficult to pursue. Confidentiality means that it should not be possible for anyone outside the research team to identify any of the participants. The practice that *"no one will be able to identify the participants in the study"* is known as the term anonymity.
- Informed consent: This is a duty of the researcher. The purpose of this is to inform subjects about the nature and purpose of the experiment, and to give the subject a sufficient amount of time to consider whether he or she wants to participate. A difficultly of stipulation might occur when the researcher has to decide how much detail to pass on to the subjects. The informed consent created for the experiment of this Master's thesis is attached to the appendix.
- Conduct of the researcher: Throughout the whole experiment, the researcher should make sure that data collected form participants is kept private.
- Internet based research: Data collected through internet based research studies raises some particular issues, since it is possible that participants be identifies though their IP address, or that third party might be able to get access to data that is stored in a database. For this thesis, an online experiment was conducted. All data was stored in a database. The database is password protected so that data is locked form third party access. Therefore, data privacy can be ensured.

The following data quality dimensions were included in the research: accuracy, timeliness, completeness, appropriate amount, interpretability, ease of understanding, representational consistency, concise representation, and relevancy. Previous research has mainly looked at the dimensions accuracy, timeliness, and completeness. This thesis is an extension of frameworks used and tested in prior studies.

Lee et al. (2006, pp. 27-66) describe methods for assessing subjective and objective data quality as a comparative approach. Subjective data quality can be measured with using the Information Quality Assessment (IAQ) survey. The survey is based on a Likert-scale ranging from 0 to 10, whereas "0" indicates "not at all" and "10" indicates "completely". The survey ascertains a participant's role (data collector, data custodian, data consumer), the dimensional quality of information, how knowledgeable a respondent is in regard to the data quality environment in the company (e.g. data quality problems), how knowledgeable a participant is in regard to the collection, the usage, and the processing of data, background information about the respondent, and respondents' importance ratings of the different data quality dimensions. The results of the Information Quality Assessment (IAQ) survey demonstrate subjective data quality ratings across the roles of data collectors, data custodians, and data consumers.

In this study, participants were assigned the role of data consumers. Data custodians and data collectors have not been considered and compared against each other. Instead, different groups of subjects have been created to determine differences in decision-making efficiency. This fits better to the goals of the thesis.

4.3 Experimental Procedure

In total, there were five different treatment groups, each with the same scenario, but with different levels of data quality. For each treatment group, there was a brief introduction given on the front page of the online experiment. The introduction included an invitation to participate in the study, an explanation of what the experiment was about, as well as a confidentiality statement that informed the subjects that no personal identifiers would be used and that all data stored would remain confidential (informed consent). An agreement to the terms and conditions of the informed consent was necessary to participate in the study.

On the second and the third page of the online experiment, participants were given a brief explanation about what they needed to do in the online simulation. Participants had to take over the role of an operations manager in a manufacturing company and order the amount of beer bottles that best fit future demands. Before starting the experiment to make the predictions, subjects were presented the goal of their task, which was to make as much profit as possible by trying to order to exact amount of beer bottles needed. Ordering too many items would result in inventory costs, composed of fixed inventory holding costs and variable costs incurred by each beer bottle that needed to be stored. Ordering too few items would result in additional costs incurred by unsatisfied customers. Meeting the exact amount of demanded bottles would lead to the highest possible profit. In general, the scenario represented a simple inventory management system in which participants had to make decisions based on information given about past demand of beer bottles.

A variation of graphs and tables was used in the experiment to simulate different levels of data quality. In addition, some of the information was replaced by erroneous data, some other information was not shown on purpose in order to create the impression of incomplete data. In total, five different treatment groups were created. Data was manipulated for each of the five groups, with the assumption that data quality perceptions would differ from group to group, and that different perceptions would have an influence on decision-making efficiency. The treatment groups will be described later in this chapter.

Subjects were asked to click through the scenario, analyze the data that was presented to them, and make a decision on what they thought the demand of beer bottles would be for three consecutive months. There were three rounds in which subjects' performance was recorded. In the subsequent part of the experiment, participants were invited to answer questions that were taken and adjusted from the Information Quality Assessment Survey (IQA). The purpose of this was to measure perceived dimensions of data quality. There were 41 questions in total assessing nine different dimensions. At the very end of the online simulation, subjects were asked to provide demographic information like age, their occupation, what their major was (optional), their gender, as well as any tools used that might have aided them in making decisions within the experimental setting.

4.3.1 Scenario and Tasks

As Harvey (2001: 59-64) already mentioned, forecasting involves the assessment of uncertainty, as well as the adjustment and evaluation of forecasts. Judgments in forecasting may be improved by a variety of techniques. *"Studying data in graphical rather than in tabular form when making judgmental forecasts"* is one of the principles for improving forecasting performance of humans. It has been proven that forecasts based on graphical representation of trend data are more accurate than forecasts based on data that is presented in a table.

The figure below shows how past demand data was displayed to participants within one of the five control groups in the online experiment. The assumption is that subjects are able to improve their decision-making performance for the tasks they needed to accomplish in the scenario with the support of graphs.

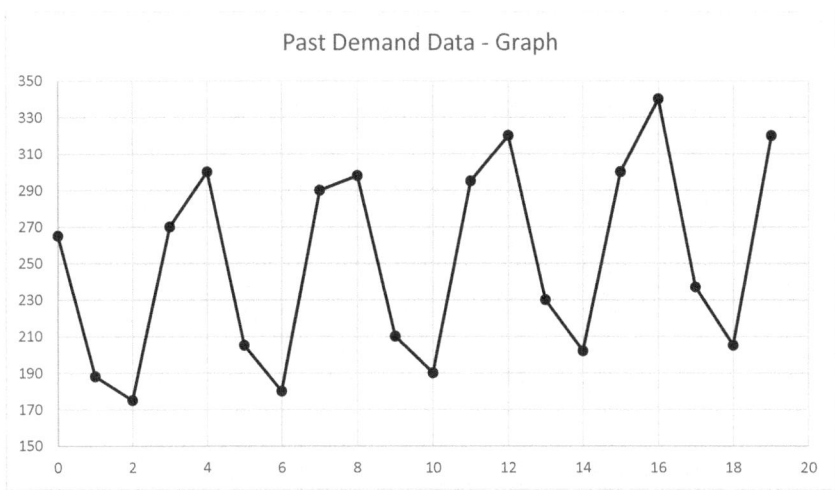

Figure 8: Graphical representation of past demand data in the experiment

Data was presented differently in each of the treatment groups. An example of data, which was the same as on the graph before, but presented in tabular form, is shown below.

2011

January	February	March	April	May	June	July	August	September	October	November	December
				265	188	175	270	300	205	180	290

2012

January	February	March	April	May	June	July	August	September	October	November	December
298	210	190	295	320	230	202	300	340	237	205	320

Figure 9: Data presented in tabular form

All data points given (demand data) had the same value for each of the groups. Each value on the data series was calculated from a trend function that was not visible to respondents. The data points for the three values that participants had to forecast were already known before. Therefore, the decision support system that respondents were using was meant to simulate a deterministic environment. The optimal values for the three future demand data points are shown in the table below.

Year	Month	Demand Value
2011	May	265
	June	188
	July	175
	August	270
	September	300
	October	205
	November	180
	December	290
2012	January	298
	February	210
	March	190
	April	295
	May	320
	June	230
	July	202
	August	300
	September	340
	October	237
	November	205
	December	320

In the table below, the three optimal values participants had to estimate are depicted. The trend function for calculating these values can be found in the appendix. The values from the table above are based on the same function.

Year	Month	Optimal Demand Value
2013	January	343
	February	249
	March	229

As an example, participants were asked to forecast future demand for January 2013 based on the data they were given in the scenario. Forecasting the exact same value as the optimal value would result in the highest profit within the scenario of the simulated inventory management system.

4.3.2 Independent Variables

Nine different data quality dimensions were measured with using and adjusting items from the Information Quality Assessment Survey (Wang & Strong, 1996):

- Accuracy: *"The degree to which data correctly reflects the real world object"* or *"an event being described"* (executionmih, n.d.: online).
- Relevancy: Data is relevant when it is applicable, interesting, and usable.
- Timeliness: An example of data which is not timely can be explained with a courier package status change in a batch processing system. A change of status in reality might not be reflected immediately in the batch processing system, since it might take one day to update the status (executionmih, n.d.: online).
- Completeness: Data can be considered complete even though not all data is available. Data completeness refers to the *"extend to which the expected attributes of data are provided"* (executionmih, n.d.: online).
- Amount of data
- Interpretability
- Ease of understanding: If data is readable and clear to its consumers, it can be considered easy to understand.
- Representational consistency: This is data which is continuously presented in the same format, consistently represented and formatted, as well as compatible with data that was presented previously.

- Concise representation: Well-presented, well-organized, aesthetically pleasing, well-formatted data is concise in its representation.

These dimensions were picked based on ease of testing them in an online experiment, and a judgment made for the testability of items in a deterministic environment. Therefore, some of the items from the survey could not be included in the research. As an example, accuracy can be simulated by injecting visual errors into data. This might alter people's perceptions of data accuracy. On the other hand, objectivity of data would require a real data source, or accessibility of data would require a simulation in which data be secured against unauthorized access, so that all users will not be able to access the same information at the same time. An inclusion of data quality dimensions that could not be tested in this experiment is suggested for future research.

Gender, age, and whether or not somebody was primarily a student were as well taken into account as independent variables. Whether participants had used any type of supporting tools like calculators or paper and pen was added as independent variables atop of the aforementioned ones.

4.3.3 Dependent Variables

There were two dependent variables that were tested in the web-based experiment:
- Time for making a decision: This was measured in seconds, and was recorded in the background. Participants were not told that time was measured in the experiment, since this could have had an impact on the results. In total, there were three estimations that participants had to make. The time passed for making estimations was stored, and added to the total amount of time that it took for respondents to complete the whole scenario.
- Decision-making performance: This was measured in terms of total profit that participants were able to make in the scenario. More accurate estimations would have a positive effect on profit, whereas less accurate estimations would lower profit.

4.3.4 Control Variables

There might be variables that are difficult or even impossible to include in the research, but these variables could hypothetically have an influence on the results:
- Need for cognition: According to Cacioppo & Petty (1982), this is *"the tendency for an individual to engage in and enjoy thinking"*. There is evidence that the probability of organizing, elaborating on, and evaluating information is higher for individuals with a high need for cognition.

- Self-efficacy: People make judgments about the degree to which they believe that they are capable of performing particular tasks (Axtell & Parker, 2003). This could mean that individuals might reject participation in the online experiment because of low self-efficacy. Therefore, most of the respondents could be individuals with high self-efficacy.
- Other variables like the time or patience that somebody has for completing the experiment might as well deliver distortion in the results. Participants were asked to ensure that they had enough time for the online simulation. They were also recommended to eliminate disturbances that might distract them from completing any of the tasks in the scenario.

4.3.5 Treatment Groups

Participants were randomly assigned into one of five groups. For each group, data was presented differently. The idea behind that was to artificially create different perceptions of data quality, and to measure time and decision making performance between these groups so that insight could be generated which would help answering the research questions stated in chapter 3 (research questions and hypotheses). A short description for each of the designed groups is given below, a detailed view of the groups is available in the appendix.

Group 1
The series of demand data in the first group was presented in tabular form only. None of the data records were flawed. The intention of creating this group was to have no errors in the data, so that participants might find it easier to make predictions than in other groups.

Group 2
The purpose of this group was to alter perceptions of data quality in terms of data completeness. Like in the first group, data was presented in tabular form, but with half of the data points missing. As an example, for the month of May 2011, "no data" was available for the participant, whereas 188 was presented as the demand data for beer bottles for the month after that.

Group 3
The idea behind the third group was to present the data points both in tabular form and as a graph. There were no discrepancies in terms of the values of data shown on each of the figures. Data were only presented in a different format. The graph might support the decision maker for improving judgment, but at the same time the amount of data is higher than in other groups. This could lead to a different perception of the amount of data.

Group 4
The difference between this group and the previous one is that half of the data points were missing, both in the table and on the graph. The assumption here is that data that is less complete can be compensated by a graphical representation of the data available, even though data suffers from incompleteness.

Group 5
In this group, data was only presented in tabular form. The difference to the other groups is that some of the demand data points were flawed. In addition, there was an indicator of how accurate data was for each of the data points, shown as percentage. As an example, demand for August 2011 was 270, with 90% accuracy of the data collected, whereas demand for November 2011 contained an error. "180r" is intended to invoke a different perception of data accuracy. The lack of data accuracy was also indicated with a reduction in the percentage (80%). For each of the percentages, there was a tolerance of +/- 5% in data accuracy, e.g. 90% +/- 5%. The results for how displaying data quality measures atop of demand data are presented in the chapter 5 (results).

5 Results

To test the hypotheses presented in chapter 3 (research questions and hypotheses), data was collected from the experiment, which was conducted with students at University of Nebraska Omaha and Management Center Innsbruck, as well as people reached through Facebook, and employees from an Omaha-based accounting firm. A multiple linear regression analysis was performed to see whether data quality and additional variables have an influence on decision-making performance as well as the time it takes to make a decision. According to Yan & Gang Su (2009: 41) as well as Freund, Wilson & Sa (2006: 73), multiple linear regression is used to investigate the relationship between more than one independent variables and a dependent variable. This is ideal for this study, since nine data quality dimensions are included as independent variables.

87 complete responses could be collected from the data gathering process. 61 participants were male and 26 were female. 55 out of the 87 stated to primarily be a student. A distribution of age ranges is illustrated in the graph below.

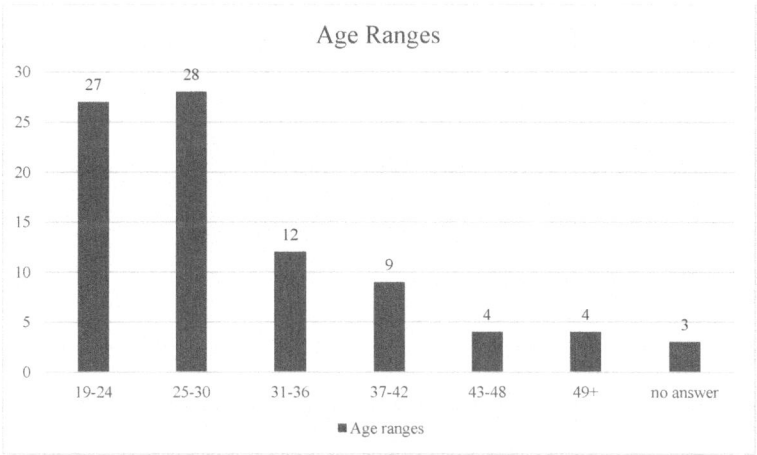

Figure 10: Age range distribution

On average, participants needed 259 seconds for the estimation part of the experiment, whereby 17 seconds was the lowest amount of time that somebody took, and 1716 was the highest. The average profit respondents could make was 385, with a minimum of negative 7994, and a maximum of 1606. Below are two graphs that show minimum, mean, and maximum amount of time as well as profit for each of the five control groups in the experiment.

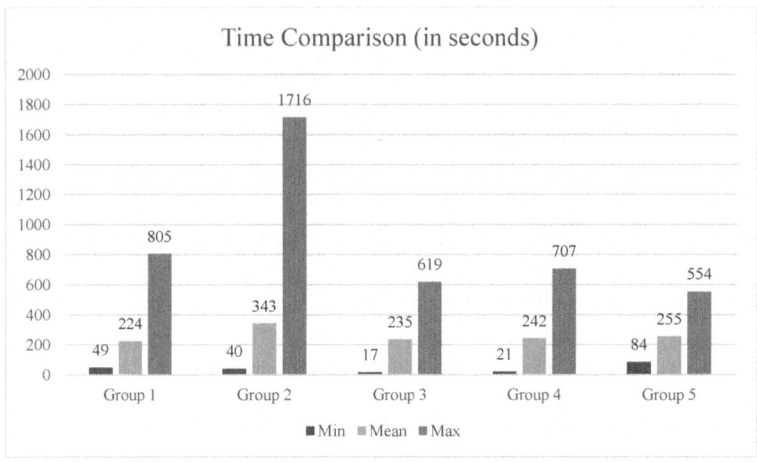

Figure 11: Time comparisons between groups

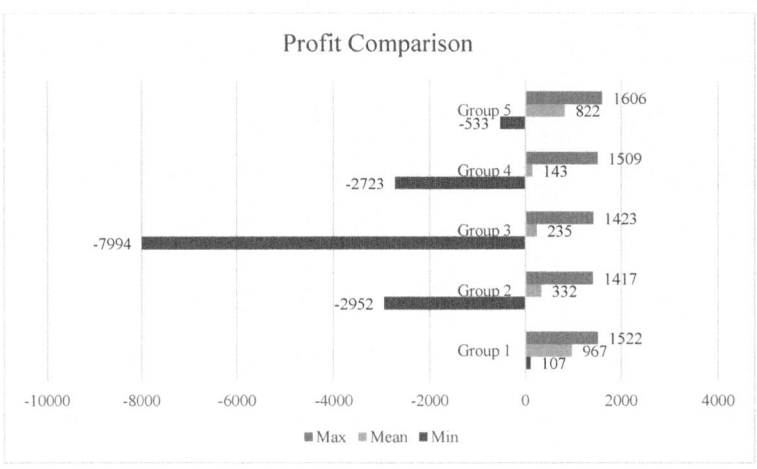

Figure 12: Profit comparisons between groups

Data quality perceptions in the five different groups may differ. Calculating the average mean for each of the data quality dimensions and comparing them between the groups brings the following results (graph below).

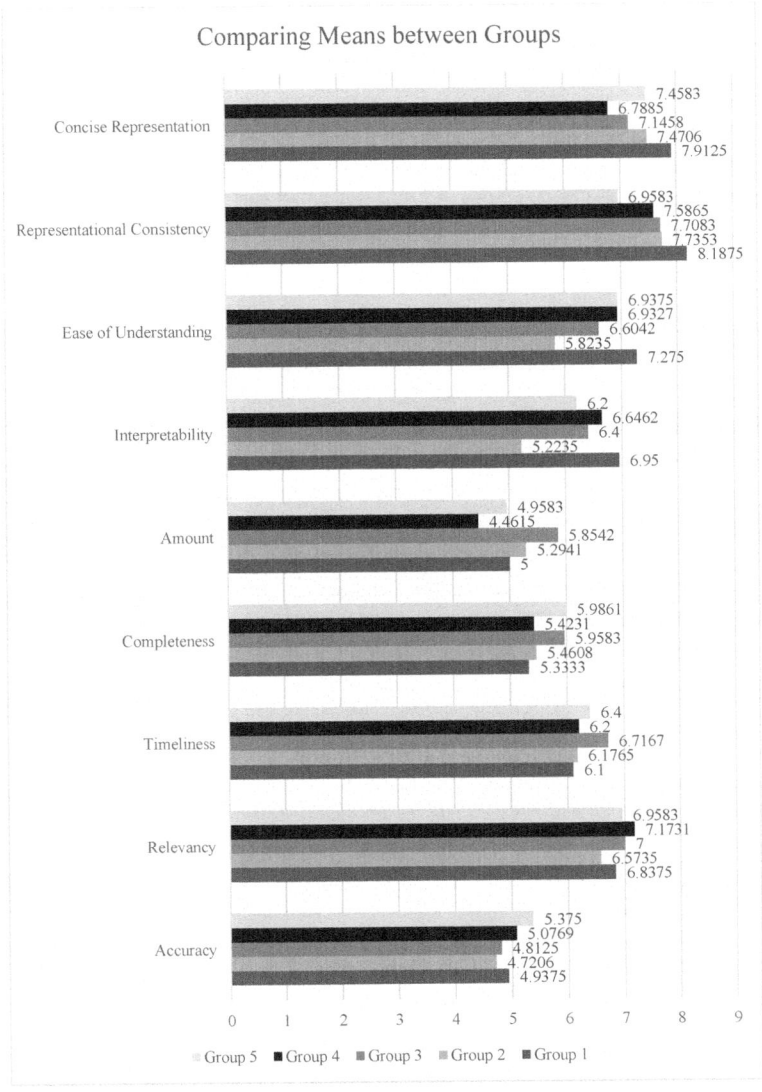

Figure 13: Comparing data quality dimension means between groups

By conducting a MANOVA across all nine data quality dimensions for all five groups, one can see whether there are any group-specific differences in regards to the mean values. Both Pillai's Trace and Wilks' Lambda are higher than .05 (p = .066 for Pillai's Trace and p = .062 for Wilks' Lambda). This means that there are no perceived difference between the groups set up in the experiment. Even when performing single ANOVA's for each of the dimensions separately, no differences between the groups can be identified. The reason for this could be that the scenario was based on the same information and design throughout the entire experiment. It might be surprising that no differences in data completeness between the five groups could be noticed, even though for two of the groups, only half of the data records were available. This needs further investigation. In the upcoming text, there will be a detailed analysis for each of the five research questions.

RQ1

In order to test the influence of data quality on one's performance of making decisions, a multiple linear regression was conducted for each of the dependent variables (time and performance).

The results show an R^2 of .187 for the time, which means that 18.7% of the total variation in time can be accounted for by the nine independent variables of data quality. R^2 does not differ significantly from 0 (p = 0.054 and, thus, is greater than .05). This means that data quality might not have an influence on the time it takes to make a decision. This is at least what the results tell us for this experiment. H_1 can therefore not be rejected. Furthermore, one can tell from the results that accuracy and the amount of data have an effect on the dependent variable time (with p = .041 < .05 for accuracy, and p = .05 <= .05 for the amount of data). The regression equation for predicting the time (in seconds) can be written as follows:

$$Total\ time\ (t) = 612.082 - 74.173\ (accuracy) + 23.067\ (relevancy) + .99\ (timeliness)$$
$$+ 22.95\ (completeness) - 49.25\ (amount\ of\ data) - 40.024\ (interpretability)$$
$$+ 5.973\ (ease\ of\ understanding) + 34.721\ (representational\ consistency)$$
$$- 11.505\ (concise\ representation)$$

From this regression equation, one can read that data accuracy influences time the most. Increasing data accuracy by one unit, time could be reduced by 74.173 seconds. Maybe complementary to Chan's (2001) study, who proved that information overload (increased amount of information) leads to a reduction in decision-making performance, the results of this Master's thesis tell that increasing the amount of data (within the scenario set up for the experiment) decreases time as well. This could probably be explained by having a graph in addition to information which is presented in tabular form is more information than the table only, but it might fit participant's cognition such that time is reduced and faster decisions can be made. Another explanation could be that participants might only be looking for information on the graph, without even considering the table. It may be doubted that amount of information and time are linearly related in general, but it might be the case within a certain context (e.g. within the experiment for this study), or within certain levels of information load. As an example, results may be different if the information load is being increased drastically.

For decision-making performance, R^2 equates to .174, which means that 17.4% of the total variation in decision-making performance (profit) can be explained by the nine independent variables of data quality. Again, R^2 does not differ significantly from 0 (p = .081 > 0.05). Hence, H_2 cannot be rejected as well. It seems as if data quality is not a predictor for decision-making performance, since representational consistency is the only independent variable that has a significant influence on decision-making performance (p = .025 < 0.05). The regression equation for predicting decision-making performance in terms of profit is as follows:

$$Performance = -1189.7 + 63.661\ (accuracy) - 131.061\ (relevancy) - 116.603\ (timeliness) + 138.254\ (completeness) - 173.283\ (amount\ of\ data) + 140.451\ (interpretability) + 49.901\ (ease\ of\ understanding) + 278.443\ (representational\ consistency) - 50.706\ (concise\ representation)$$

From the equation, one can infer that increasing accuracy of data (eliminating errors) by one unit increases performance by 63.661 units. The biggest contributor to improving decision-making performance is representational consistency. Increasing this dimension by one unit leads to an increase of performance of 278.443 units.

It may be surprising that only one dimension of data quality is responsible for a change in decision-making efficiency, but this behavior can probably be related to a human's ability to compensate information of poor quality with certain information processing skills. It may be the case that compensating poor data quality takes place by more time that is consumed in the decision-making process for making a prediction.

RQ2

As a next step, more variables were added to the regression analysis. Age, gender, occupation, and supporting tools used for making predictions might change the outcome of the study. Considering the dependent variable time, the additional independent variables cause R^2 to be higher than before (R^2 = .301). 30.1% of the total variation of data quality can be accounted for by all nine data quality dimensions as well as factors such as age, occupation, gender, and supporting tools used. Now that p equals .015, one can infer that R^2 differs significantly from 0 (p < .05), which means that considering the additional variables atop of data quality, an impact on decision-making efficiency in terms of time can be noticed. Thus, H_3 can be rejected. In addition to the amount of data and data accuracy, using paper and pen to support estimation tasks affects decision-making efficiency as well (p = .047 < .05). Increasing accuracy by one unit decreases the amount of time it takes to make a decision by 98.672 seconds. Increasing the amount of data by one unit decreases time by 71.162 seconds. Using paper and pen instead of not using it leads to a time increase of 161.748 units. The regression equation for including age, occupation, gender, and used tools looks like this:

$$\begin{aligned}Total\ time\ (t) = {} & 802.345 - 98.672\ (accuracy) + 26.56\ (relevancy) + 2.619\ (timeliness) \\ & + 25.676\ (completeness) - 71.162\ (amount\ of\ data) - 50.685\ (interpretability) \\ & + 24.38\ (ease\ of\ understanding) + 25.083\ (representational\ consistency) \\ & - 13.416\ (concise\ representation) + 52.865\ (gender) - 27.075\ (age) \\ & + 40.004\ (student) + 49.342\ (calculator\ used) + 161.748\ (paper\ and\ pen\ used)\end{aligned}$$

Regarding decision-making performance, one can derive from the results that 24.2% of the total variation in performance can be accounted for by a variation of the nine independent data quality dimensions, as well as the variables age, gender, occupation, and tools used to support decision making (R^2 = .242). The fact that p equals .088 means performance is not influenced by the variables considered in the analysis and, thus, H_4 cannot be rejected.

$$\begin{aligned}Performance = {} & -836.339 + 122.701\ (accuracy) - 235.78\ (relevancy) - 136.162\ (timeliness) \\ & + 130.792\ (completeness) - 146.542\ (amount\ of\ data) + 146.205\ (interpretability) \\ & + 63.054\ (ease\ of\ understanding) + 262.65\ (representational\ consistency) \\ & - 3.787\ (concise\ representation) + 628.47\ (gender) - 110.292\ (age) \\ & - 347.743\ (student) - 364.247\ (calculator\ used) - 310.155\ (paper\ and\ pen\ used)\end{aligned}$$

Again, the results show that representational consistency is the only factor that has an effect on decision-making performance. Increasing it by one unit would increase performance by 262.65 units. In the previous test (addressing the time it takes to make a decision as a dependent variable), using paper and pen as supporting tools has a positive relation to decision-making time, but it would not change performance. A more detailed analysis is recommended. One could use the independent samples t-test in order to find out whether subjects with supporting tools performed better in the scenario than subjects who did not use any tool. According to SPSS, the p-value for the 2-tailed Sigma is .403, which means that the null-hypothesis that using paper and pen does not make a difference in terms of decision-making performance can be rejected. In fact, subjects who used paper and pen could get remarkably better results (average mean = 438.55) than subjects who did not use any of these tools (average mean = 52.67). The question is why there is such a huge difference between these groups. One explanation could be that humans tend to learn best from using visuals rather than from just reading information. Another explanation could be that when using paper and pen to support estimation tasks, subjects are more likely to encounter a cognitive fit of information.

RQ 3
Research question four addresses participants' learnability rate of decision-making tasks within the same environment, and with conducting similar tasks within a relatively short amount of time. The assumption is that humans learn from their mistakes so that they will make better decisions in the future. For this purpose, one can perform a paired samples t-test for comparing the means of decision-making performance between two items within one group. The t-test is 2-tailed, which means a deviation from the mean to either side of the distribution curve will be considered, with the assumption that the mean is the optimal amount for demand data for each month simulated in the experiment. As an example, 343 would be the optimal amount to estimate for the first month. In other words, profit or decision-making performance would be best then. In order to be as accurate as possible, one has to measure the delta between optimal amount and estimated amount. This will show participants' actual performance in the experiment. In part one of this investigation, one can compare estimations made for task one and estimations made for task two. Part two includes comparing task two performance and task three performance.

The average mean for task one estimations is 75.48, which is calculated from the mean of the absolute values of the deviation of the ideal value (343). Analogously, 86.49 is the average deviation from the optimal value of participants for tasks two, and 125.1 for task three. This means that even though participants encountered the execution of similar tasks and had the possibility to learn from previous experience, their performance seemed to go down. In order to scientifically prove this, one needs to conduct a t-test for paired samples. The results show that for the first part of the testing, p equals .165, which means that, with a confidence interval of 95%, H_5 cannot be rejected. Participants' performance can be deemed as good in task two as in task one. P for the second part of the testing is below .05 (p = .03). This means that H_6 can be rejected. Participants' performance for making estimations decreased after the second round. 156 second was the average amount of time it took for participants to perform the estimations for task one, 57 seconds for task two, and 46 seconds for task three. Conducting a paired samples t-test on time, with a 95% confidence interval, shows that the times for each of the tasks differ (p for task one and two = 0, and p for task two and three = .01). Even though respondents took the same amount of time for both task two and three, they performed worse in task three than in task two. The assumption that there is a learning effect for making consecutive predictions within similar settings can therefore not be confirmed. It might have been the case that, even in this simulated deterministic environment, participants got influenced by the feedback that was provided to them after making estimations. For example, respondents in the experiment would receive information telling them how much profit they made after each round, and how close they were to the actual value.

RQ4

There might be a tradeoff between the time it takes to make a decision and decision-making performance, as suggested by Vessey (1991), Kuo et al. (2004), and Davern & Kamis (2010). In order to gain insight about tradeoff issues related to making predictions, one needs to determine the Pearson Product-Moment Correlation Coefficient (for metric correlations) between the variables time and performance. This will help to determine causalities between these two factors. In addition, a bivariate regression analysis can be conducted to determine the linear correlations between variables when the independent and dependent variable is known. P (2-tailed) is .355, which means that H_7 cannot be rejected. There is no linear relationship between time and performance for the overall scenario. In this case, conducting a bivariate regression analysis is obsolete. One can look into analyzing the correlations between factors for each of the tasks (partial analysis of correlations). For task one, there is no linear correlation existing between time and performance. Therefore, H_8 cannot be rejected as well (2-tailed p = .356). For task two, p (2-tailed) equates to .533, and for task three, p (2-tailed) is .22, with a coefficient of .068 and negative .133 each. Again, H_9 and H_{10} cannot be rejected. There is no linear relationship existing between time and performance for neither of the three estimation tasks.

A probable explanation of this behavior might be that decision-making performance is primarily dependent on participants' cognitive ability to make predictions, no matter how much time respondents consume to give estimations about future demand. It could be that even though one needs more time to make a decision than another person, both can still get the same results. Another scenario might be that some people might need the same amount of time, but their performance varies. This could probably all be related to one's self-efficacy (Axtell & Parker, 2003) and need for cognition (Cacioppo & Petty, 1982), which, due to complexity of the experiment, could not be taken into account for this study (see control variables under 4.3.4).

RQ5

In order to determine whether gender, age, occupation, or tools used (paper and pen as well as calculator) are variables that have an impact on how data quality is perceived, different statistical tests are necessary. For analyzing the influence of gender on perceived data quality, an independent samples t-test can be performed.

Gender and Perceived Data Quality

According to the results of an independent t-test for each of the data quality dimensions, perceived data timeliness, data completeness, and amount of data are influenced by gender. The average mean for each of these dimensions is higher for males than it is for females. The p-values for these dimensions are lower than .05 and, therefore, the null-hypotheses for the individual parts of the overall hypothesis can be rejected for a confidence interval of 95%. The null-hypothesis for checking whether gender influences data quality as a whole can be rejected as well after executing a MANOVA (H_{11} = rejected). Pillai's Trace as well as Wilks' Lambda have a p-value of .016 (p < .05). The Partial Eta Squared is .224, which can be expressed as 22.4% of the total variation of perceived data quality is being accounted for by a variation in gender.

The fact that perceived data quality can differ between males and females needs further investigation. It could be that men and women differ in the ability to process certain amounts of data. This could be a discussion for further research.

Occupation and Perceived Data Quality

None of the data quality dimensions that were included in the experiment are impacted in any form by one's occupation. The p-values for all variables are above .05 (p = .233) and, thus, the means of all data quality dimensions do not differ between participants whose primary occupation is student and participants whose primary occupation is other than student. Therefore, H_{12} cannot be rejected.

Age and Perceived Data Quality

A MANOVA is necessary to determine whether there are perceived data quality level differences between more than two age groups. The means of all nine data quality dimensions will be compared against each other.

According to the results gained from SPSS, the null-hypothesis H_{13} that data quality dimensions are perceived the same across all classifications of age can be rejected, since both Pillai's Trace and Wilks' Lambda have a p-value lesser than .05, with p = .026 for Pillai's Trace and p = .02 for Wilks' Lambda. Partial Eta Squared is .144, which means that about 14.4% of variability in perceived data quality across all nine dependent variables is being accounted for by a variation of the six age groups tested. This approach combines all dependent variables and, thus, the null-hypothesis can be rejected for the combination of all data quality dimensions. Looking at the individual dependent variables separately with performing ANOVA's, age-specific differences can be discovered for the dimensions relevancy and completeness (p for relevancy = .004 and p for completeness = .009).

Using a Calculator
Some of the participants have used paper and pen to aid their estimations, even though it was not a requirement for the experiment to use any supporting tools. This could probably have an effect on some of the independent variables of data quality. Therefore, one needs to ensure that these factors are taken into consideration as well. In order to statistically prove any relationships between the usage of paper and pen and data quality, one can conduct a MANOVA. SPSS shows a p-value for both Pillai's Trace and Wilks' Lambda of .633, which means that the null-hypotheses H_{14} that using a calculator does not have an impact on perceived data quality dimensions cannot be rejected. Looking at each of the data quality dimensions individually with performing single ANOVA's on each of the items results in p-values that are all above .05, confirming the assumption that using a calculator does not influence someone's perception of data accuracy, data completeness, data timeliness, etc.

Using Paper and Pen
Some of the respondents have used a paper and pen for determining future demand values of beer bottles in the scenarios. This part of hypotheses testing is very similar to the previous testing (using calculator). It also includes the execution of a MANOVA. From the results of the statistical test, one can tell that the null-hypothesis H_{15} for testing the influence of using paper and pen on perceived data quality cannot be rejected, since p = .091 and is thus greater than .05 (Pillai's Trace and Wilks' Lambda). Looking at each of the nine quality dimensions separately, one can see that only "ease of understanding" is influenced by using paper and pen. This needs more testing, since it could be that a bad understanding of data that is presented in various formats could cause participants to use paper and pen (for better understanding and for aiding purposes). This behavior could represent the ballpark for mangers who are using supporting tools like visual boards or notebooks for improving decision-making performance. It might be more efficient and handy to draw some numbers on a piece of paper, instead of making guesses intuitively.

Below is a table that summarizes the results in regards to the hypotheses stated in chapter 3 – research questions and hypotheses.

H_1: The variables accuracy, timeliness, completeness, appropriate amount, interpretability, ease of understanding, representational consistency, concise representation, and relevancy of	Not rejected

information have no influence on the time it takes to make a decision.	
H_2: The variables accuracy, timeliness, completeness, appropriate amount, interpretability, ease of understanding, representational consistency, concise representation, and relevancy of information have no influence on decision-making performance.	Not rejected
H_3: The variables accuracy, timeliness, completeness, appropriate amount, interpretability, ease of understanding, representational consistency, concise representation, relevancy, age, occupation, and supporting tools used have no influence on the time it takes to make a decision.	Rejected
H_4: The variables accuracy, timeliness, completeness, appropriate amount, interpretability, ease of understanding, representational consistency, concise representation, relevancy, age, occupation, and supporting tools used of information have no influence on decision-making performance.	Not rejected
H_5: μ decision-making performance in task one = μ decision-making performance in task two.	Not rejected
H_6: μ decision-making performance in task two = μ decision-making performance in task three.	Rejected
H_7: There is no linear relationship between decision-making performance and the time it takes to make a decision for the overall scenario.	Not rejected
H_8: There is no linear relationship between decision-making performance	Not rejected

and the time it takes to make a decision for task one.	
H_9: There is no linear relationship between decision-making performance and the time it takes to make a decision for task two.	Not rejected
H_{10}: There is no linear relationship between decision-making performance and the time it takes to make a decision for task three.	Not rejected
H_{11}: μ perceived data quality males = μ perceived data quality females.	Rejected
H_{12}: μ perceived data quality students = μ perceived data quality non-students.	Not rejected
H_{13}: Data quality is perceived the same across six different age groups.	Rejected
H_{14}: There is no relationship between using a calculator for supporting estimations and perceived data quality.	Not rejected
H_{15}: There is no relationship between using paper and pen for supporting estimations and perceived data quality.	Not rejected

Factor Analysis

A validation of the Information Quality Assessment Survey (IQAS) is also part of this thesis. In total, 41 items were picked from this survey, and adapted to the scenario developed for the experiment so that data quality dimensions could be quantified. A factor analysis will be conducted to see whether any of the items used in the study can be eliminated from future research efforts.

The aim of factor analysis is to *"summarize the interrelationships among the variables in a concise but accurate manner as an aid in conceptualization"*. Often, a maximum number of information from an original set of variables is included with as few derived variables as possible. This is because scientist follow the common goal of summarizing data such that humans are able to grasp empirical relationships among sets of data (Gorsuch, 1983: 2).

The Kaiser-Meyer-Olkin Measure of Sampling Adequacy determines if it is even appropriate to conduct a factor analysis so that items can be reduced. SPSS shows a value of .903, which means that conducting a factor analysis is adequate, since the value is greater than .5 (common limit among scientists). Nine factors were assumed to be included in the factor analysis, since nine data quality dimensions were tested. Variables with an extracted communality factor of less than .5 can be excluded from the questionnaire. The results are that one item can be eliminated from the set (item 28: "The information is not sufficiently timely", from: dimension timeliness).

A discussion about the results of this study, along with implications of the study on organizations, is presented in the next chapter. Finally, there will be conclusion in the last chapter of this paper, including limitations of this thesis as well as recommendations on future research.

sion

of the thesis, implications of the results on organizations will be
g with recommendations on how data quality could be improved in
ies. In the beginning, there will be a discourse about implications of this
thesis o.   orrow's organizations. In the second part of this chapter, the term data
quality management will be explained and how it relates to the findings of this thesis.

6.1 Implications of the Study

The major finding of the study is that data accuracy as well as the amount of data can be considered having an effect on the time it takes to make a decision. Previous research suggests that accuracy of information plays a vital role in the decision-making process. Representational consistency can be deemed having an impact on decision-making performance. It might be surprising that whenever participants used paper and pen to make estimations, their performance during the experiment increased. Using a calculator seems to not cause any effects. Using paper and pen produces remarkably better results, and it seems as if participants were able to make information fit to their intellect so that they could make better decisions.

The results of the study demonstrate the importance of data quality dimensions, in that decision-making performance and the time period for making decisions can be improved if data accuracy, and representational consistency of data be improved. The implication for companies is to ensure that data from various sources are accurate. Especially, if companies use some form of business intelligence system, actions should be taken to present data in a consistent format throughout the whole process in which data is being consumed. It is important to define a uniform format for all data that is to be included from various data sources. It is also essential that decision support systems or any other type of management information systems being used in a company are designed such that data is presented consistently and in the same format.

6.2 Data Quality Management

Ryu, Park & Park (2006) have empirically proven that the introduction of data quality management improves data quality. The authors define a data quality architecture model, in which data quality can be seen from an independent point of view (e.g. comprehensiveness, accuracy), and from an enterprise point of view (e.g. singularity, reusability). Moreover, the scholars proposed a data quality management maturity model, which can be used to manage data quality in an organization. The purpose of the model is to show where a company is currently at in terms (present state). Furthermore, it shows essential lists for devel[oped at a] higher level.

From a technical perspective, there are a number of steps a com[pany can take once] quality problems have been identified (Geiger, 2004: online):

- Exclude the data: Removing sets of data should only be [done if the] problem is considered severe.
- Accept the data: This can be done if the data is within a defined range of tolerance.
- Correct the data: Selecting a data record to be the master is recommended whenever there are variations of data in the database. Otherwise, it might be difficult to consolidate the data.
- Insert a default value: Instead of having no value for a field, it is sometimes more important to have a default value, even if the correct value is unknown or cannot be determined correctly.

Data quality management from a business perspective is a process comprising activities such as establishing and deploying roles, responsibilities, and procedures with the purpose of acquiring, maintaining, disseminating, and disposing data. Data quality management efforts are only successful if IT and business work together. Ultimately, the business areas are driving data quality, in that they are defining the business rules for governing data as well as verifying data quality. IT is responsible for setting up the environment in which data can be managed. The environment entails the architecture, the technical facilities, the systems, as well as the databases (Geiger, 2004: online).

...udy as well as recommendations for future ...port systems are successful and managers can ... when information is accurate and presented in a ... mat. The major objectives of this study were to investigate the relationship between data quality and decision-making efficiency, to find out if humans are able to improve their capability to make predictions within a short time period, to make recommendations for how to improve data quality, and find out what the most important dimensions of data quality are. The conclusion is that there are dimensions of data quality that can have an effect on decision-making efficiency and the time it takes to make a decision. In regards to data accuracy, results emanating from previous research studies could be confirmed. Poor data accuracy is probably the main cause for poor data quality, even though there are other data quality dimensions that are known to have an impact on decisions managers make.

For making recommendations towards better data accuracy, businesses must first recognize that *"data quality and consistency are a joint responsibility"*. Furthermore, creating data quality standards has to be followed by working with IT in an ongoing process of continuously improving data quality (Swoyer, 2009: online).

According to Cong et al. (2007), finding automated methods for cleaning large amounts of data in databases emerged from the need of time that is wasted by clerks who clean data manually. When integrity constraints are violated, inconsistencies in a database can be the cause, especially because real-world data that is often converted into data sets that are stored in a database contain inconstancies that are often hard to prepare for. Therefore, one should develop a repair function for automatically cleaning large amounts of data. The authors developed an algorithm for treating both consistency and accuracy of data in large amounts of data sets. The data cleansing is done incrementally, and is based on data-cleansing methods.

The findings of this research project lead to the assumption that implanting data quality management principles in a company can help to improve data quality as well as organizational performance.

7.1 Limitations

One of the limitations of the study is that students from University of Nebraska Omaha and Management Center Innsbruck, as well as employees of an Omaha based accounting and technology firm were taken into account as subjects for collecting empirical data for testing the hypotheses. Beyond these and some respondents collected through

Facebook, no other participants were included in the research, which could lead to the question if results would have been different if he sample was purely randomized, or if subjects from other universities and colleges had been recruited. In addition, the total amount of subjects tested was 87, which means that the results of the study might not be rock-solid. A larger sample size, with more tests at different locations might be necessary. Other limitations of the study include the following:

- Nine out of sixteen data quality dimensions could be measured. Thus, Wang and Strong's (1996) framework could not be completely covered in the research study.
- Factors such as participants' need for cognition or one's self-efficacy were not included in the experiment due to complexity and instrumental constraints.
- A large amount of the subjects obtained extra credit for their participation. The other part of the respondents did not get any incentives. The limitation here is that tests were not conducted between these two groups, but it would have probably been another major contribution to management theories, if the effect of incentives on human decision-making had been added to the study.
- The study was conducted with fictional data, and with deterministic values for the data points participants were asked to predict.
- The design of the decision support system used for the experiment stayed the same across all treatment groups tested. Results might have been different if a different design was chosen to conduct the study. Aesthetic aspects were not covered.
- The decision support system used in the study is restrictive in nature. For making one prediction, there is an unlimited amount of choices, that is, all positive integer numbers in theory. There was no possibility to make a mistake in the experiment, since entering no value or a negative one would not work for advancing to the subsequent task.
- One' need for cognition (Cacioppo & Petty, 1982) as well as one's self-efficacy (Axtell & Parker, 2003) can have major effects on data quality. This might explain why participants in the study were not influenced by data incompleteness or some other data quality dimensions.

7.2 Further Research

One main idea for future research is to use the experiment set up for this study and test another set of subjects so that they can be added to the data sets that were obtained from the experiment. It is recommended to use the decision support system created for this study, and perform tests on different designs of it. This way, aesthetics could be taken into consideration as a potential variable that might also have an effect on decision-making efficiency. One needs to add the opportunity for subjects to make mistakes in the experiment (e.g. entering a wrong value), so that the decision support system emulates a more realistic environment. Another option is to set up an experiment in which participants are able to receive real incentives (monetary or non-monetary). In the system used for this study, poor performance does not have any consequences, and performing well might not be beneficial for participants at all. It is therefore suggested to include multiple options in future research efforts so that incentives can be included as a factor. As an example, participants could decide whether they would like to perform an estimation, or if they wanted to spend more (fictional) money on gaining data that is more accurate. Then one could investigate different decision-making types, and see what options humans choose depending on information that is presented to them. Another recommendation is to base the data points presented in the scenario on a more complex trend function so that it is more difficult for participants to make predictions.

The decision support system used in the scenario was deterministic in nature, which means that future data values are already known before. The judgment of whether a decision was good or bad is thus based on the optimal value one can guess. For future research, it is recommended to use a less restrictive, non-deterministic decision support system, and to base the quality of decisions on other factors such as human judgment. In general, a more realistic system is recommended. This way, results can be compared against each other and one can tell if decision-making behavior changes from setting to setting.

This research study is intended to be fundamental for future tests on data quality and decision-making efficiency. It provides a general framework that can be further utilized and validated. It is also suggested to extend the framework with testing one's need for cognition as well as one's self-efficacy, since this could probably explain a large portion of the total variation in data quality. For organizations seeking to improve organizational performance, the framework presented in this research study can be used to continuously improve decision-making efficiency by twisting the design of the decision support system provided. This will give companies the opportunity to focus on the outcome of their data quality management efforts.

References

Alba, J. & Hutchinson, W. (2000): Knowledge Calibration: What Consumers Know and What They Think They Know. *Journal of Consumer Research* 27(2), 123–156.

Armstrong, J. S. (ed.) (2001): Principles of Forecasting: A handbook for researchers and practitioners. Kluwer Academic.

Axtell, C. & Parker, S. (2003): Promoting role breadth self-efficacy through involvement, work redesign and training. *Human Relations* 56(1), 113–131.

Batini, C. & Scannapieco, M. (2006): Data Quality: Concepts, Methodologies and Techniques: Springer.

Berti-Équille, L., Comyn-Wattiau, I., Cosquer, M., Kedad, Z., Nugier, S. & Peralta, V. (2011): Assessment and analysis of information quality: a multidimensional model of case studies. *International Journal of Information Quality* 2(4), 300–323.

Bharati, P. & Chaudhury, A. (2004): An empirical investigation of decision-making satisfaction in web-based decision support systems. *Decision Support Systems* 37(2), 187–197.

Cacioppo, J. & Petty, R. (1982): The Need for Cognition. *Journal of Personality and Social Psychology* 42(1), 116–131.

Canadian Institute for Health Information (2009): Data Quality. URL: http://www.cihi.ca/CIHI-ext-portal/internet/en/tabbedcontent/standards+and+data+submission/data+quality/cihi021513#_Data_Quality_I n_Action [retrieved: 2013-07-14].

Cao, L. & Zhu, H. (2013): Normal Accidents: Data Quality Problems in ERP-Enabled Manufacturing. *ACM Journal of Data and Information Quality* 4(3), 11:1-11:26.

Chan, S. (2001): The use of graphs as decision aids in relation to information overload and managerial decision quality. *Journal of Information Science* 27(6), 417–425.

Cong, G., Fan, Wenfei, Geerts, Floris, Jia, X. & Ma, S. (2007): Improving Data Quality: Consistency and Accuracy. *Proceedings of the 33rd International Conference on Very Large Data Bases* September 23-27, 315–326.

Cowie, J. & Burstein, F. (2007): Quality of data model for supporting mobile decision making. *Decision Support Systems* 43(4), 1675–1683.

Crano, W. D. & Brewer, M. B. (2002): Principles and methods of social research (2nd ed.). Mahwah, NJ [u.a.]: Lawrence Erlbaum Assoc.

Curé, O. (2012): Improving the Data Quality of Drug Databases. *ACM Journal of Data and Information Quality* 4(1), 1–21.

Dasu, T. & Johnson, T. (2003): Exploratory data mining and data cleaning. New York: Wiley-Interscience.

David, M. & Sutton, C. D. (2004): Social research: The basics. London, Thousand Oaks: SAGE Publications.

Embury, S., Missier, P., Sampaio, S., Greenwood, M. & Preece, A. (2009): Incorporating Domain-Specific Information Quality Constraints into Database Queries. *ACM Journal of Data and Information Quality* 1(2), 11:1-31.

Eppler, M. & Muenzenmayer, P. (2002): Measuring Information Quality in the Web Context: A Survey of State-of-the-art instruments and an Application Methodology. *Proceedings of the 7th International Conference on Information Quality*, 187–196.

executionmih (n.d.): Data Quality Definition: What is Data Quality? URL: http://www.executionmih.com/data-quality/accuracy-consistency-audit.php [retrieved: 2013-11-08].

Fisher, C., Lauría, E., Chengalur-Smith, S. & Wang, R. (2011): Introduction to information quality. Bloomington and IN: AuthorHouse.

Forrester Consulting (2011): Trends In Data Quality And Business Process Alignment. URL: http://www.enterpriseiq.com.au/documents/whitepapers/Trends_in_Data_Quality_and_Business_Process_Alignment.pdf [retrieved: 2012-03-21].

Freund, R. J., Wilson, W. J. & Sa, P. (2006): Regression analysis (2nd ed.). Oxford: Academic.

Geiger, J. (2004): Data Quality Management: The Most Critical Initiative You Can Implement. URL: http://www2.sas.com/proceedings/sugi29/098-29.pdf [retrieved: 2013-07-14].

Gorsuch, R. L. (1983): Factor analysis (2nd ed.). Hillsdale, N.J: L. Erlbaum Associates.

Grünig, R. & Kühn, R. (2005): Successful decision making: A systematic approach to complex problems. Berlin and New York: Springer.

Harvey, N. (2001): Improving judgment in forecasting, in: Armstrong, J. S. (ed.): *Principles of Forecasting*, 59–80.

Heinrich, B. & Klier, M. (2011): Assessing data currency: a probabilistic approach. *Journal of Information Science* 37(1), 86–100.

IBM (2010): The high cost of low data quality, and solving it through improved data management. URL: ftp://public.dhe.ibm.com/common/ssi/ecm/en/sww14008usen/SWW14008USEN.PDF [retrieved: 2012-12-17].

Joglekar, N., Anderson, E. & Shankaranarayanan (2013): Accuracy of Aggregate Data in Distributed Project Settings: Model, Analysis and Implications. *ACM Journal of Data and Information Quality* 4(3), 13:1-13:22.

Johnson, R. & Levin, I. (1985): More Than Meets the Eye: The Effect of Missing Information on Purchase Evaluations. *Journal of Consumer Research* 12(2), 169–177.

Kristiano, Y., Gunasekaran, A., Helo, P. & Sandhu, M. (2012): A decision support system for integrating manufacturing and product design into the reconfiguration of the supply chain networks. *Decision Support Systems* 52(4), 790–801.

Kuo, F.-Y., Chu, T.-H., Hsu, M.-H. & Hsieh, H.-S. (2004): An investigation of effort-accuracy tradeoff and the impact of self-efficacy on Web searching behaviors. *Decision Support Systems* 37(3), 331–342.

Lee, Y. W. (2006): Journey to data quality. Cambridge and Mass: MIT Press.

Lim, J. S. & O'Connor, M. (1996): Judgmental forecasting with interactive forecasting support systems. *Decision Support Systems* 16(4), 339–357.

Lunenburg, F. (2010): The Decision Making Process. *National Forum of Educational Administration and Supervision Journal* 27(4), 1–12.

Madnick, S., Wang, R., Lee, Y. & Zhu, H. (2009): Overview and Framework for Data and Information Quality Research. *ACM Journal of Data and Information Quality* 1(1), 2:1-22.

McNaull, J., Augusto, J. C., Mulvenna, M. & McCullagh, P. (2012): Data and Information Quality Issues in Ambient Assisted Living Systems. *ACM Journal of Data and Information Quality* 4(1), 4:2-4:15.

Michael, D. & Kamis, A. (2010): Knowledge matters: Restrictiveness and performance with decision support. *Decision Support Systems* 49(4), 343–353.

Petter, S., DeLone, W. & McLean, E. (2008): Measuring information system success: models, dimensions, measures, and interrelationships. *European Journal of Information Systems* 17(17), 236–263.

Pipino, L., Lee, Y. & Wang, R. (2002): Data Quality Assessment. *Communications of the ACM* 45(4), 211–218.

Raghunathan, S. (1999): Impact of information quality and decision-maker quality on decision quality: A theoretical model and simulation analysis. *Decision Support Systems* 26(4), 275–286.

Redman, T. (1998): The Impact of Poor Data Quality on the Typical Enterprise. *Communications of the ACM* 41(2), 79–82.

Rockwell, D. (2012): 5 Tips for Cleaning Your Dirty Data. URL: http://tdwi.org/articles/2012/05/22/5-tips-cleaning-data.aspx.

Ryu, K.-S., Park, J.-S. & Park, J.-H. (2006): A Data Quality Management Maturity Model. *ETRI Journal* 28(2), 191–204.

Sabherwal, R. & Becerra-Fernandez, I. (2011): Business intelligence. Hoboken and NJ: Wiley.

Sedera, D. & Gable, G. (2004): A Factor and Structural Equation Analysis of the Enterprise Systems Success Measurement Model. *International Conference on Information Systems*.

Simmons, C. & Lynch, J. (1991): Inference Effects without Inference Making? Effects of Missing Information on Discounting and Use of Presented Information. *Journal of Consumer Research* 17(4), 447–491.

Sugumaran, R. & DeGroote, J. (2011): Spatial decision support systems: Principles and practices. Boca Raton [u.a.]: Taylor & Francis.

Swoyer, S. (2009): What Businesses Must Do to Improve Data Accuracy. URL: http://tdwi.org/articles/2009/09/30/what-businesses-must-do-to-improve-data-accuracy.aspx [retrieved: 2013-11-08].

Tee, S. W., Bowen, P. L., Doyle, P. & Rohde, F. H. (2007): Factors influencing organizations to improve data quality in their information systems. *Accounting and Finance* 47(2), 335–355.

Vessey, I. (1991): Cognitive Fit: A Theory-Based Analysis of the Graphs Versus Tables Literature. *Decision Sciences* 22(2), 219–240.

Vosburg, J. & Anil, K. (2001): Managing dirty data in organizations using ERP: lessons from a case study. *Industrial Management & Data Systems* 101(1), 21–31.

Wang, R. & Strong, D. (1996): Beyond Accuracy: What Data Quality Means to Data Consumers. *Journal of Management Information Systems* 12(4), 5–34.

Xu, H., Nord, J. H., Brown, N. & Nord, G. D. (2002): Data quality issues in implementing an ERP. *Industrial Management & Data Systems* 102(1), 47–58.

Yan, X. & Su, X. (op. 2009): Linear regression analysis: Theory and computing. Singapore and Hackensack and NJ: World Scientific.

Springer Gabler

springer-gabler.de

Das Research-Programm für Wirtschaftswissenschaften

Mit Springer Gabler publizieren Sie schnell ...
- Reputation und Aktualität durch rasche Review-Prozesse
- Online first via SpringerLink: Sofort zitierbar
- Kurze Produktionszeiten bei Druck von Ihrer PDF-Datei oder alternativ XML-Satz durch den Verlag

international ...
- In deutscher oder englischer Sprache
- Hohe wissenschaftliche Sichtbarkeit durch SpringerLink
- Seien Sie Teil des Springer-Netzes, auf das mehr als 15.000 Institutionen Zugriff haben

mehr als nur einmalig ...
- Fastline: Nutzen Sie unser Programm „Springer Gabler Results" für innovative und kompakte Forschungsbeiträge bis 120 Seiten
- E-Magazin Artikel: Wir unterstützen Sie bei der Aufwertung Ihrer Publikationsliste, indem wir Ihre Fachartikel online platzieren
- Lehrbuchautoren: Gern vermitteln wir weitere Publikationsmöglichkeiten, z.B. als Fach- oder Lehrbuchautor bei Springer DE

Kontakt für Veröffentlichungen:
Marta Schmidt
Springer Gabler | Springer Fachmedien Wiesbaden GmbH
Lektorat Research
tel +49 (0)611 / 78 78 – 237
marta.schmidt@springer.com

Werden Sie AutorIn des neuen Springer Gabler Research-Programms!

Printed by Printforce, United Kingdom